THE CRYSTAL COAST

VOICES OF AMERICA

THE CRYSTAL COAST

Compiled by
Lynn Salsi and Frances Eubanks

ARCADIA

Published by Arcadia Publishing,
an imprint of Tempus Publishing, Inc.
2 Cumberland Street
Charleston, SC 29401

Printed in Great Britain.

Library of Congress Catalog Card Number: 00-107285

For all general information contact Arcadia Publishing at:
Telephone 843-853-2070
Fax 843-853-0044
E-Mail: sales@arcadiapublishing.com

For customer service and orders:
Toll-Free 1-888-313-2665

Visit us on the internet at http://www.arcadiaimages.com

In honor of
Mrs. Nettie Willis Murrill (1911–2000)
Mrs. Clara Salter Gaskins (1917–1999)

And for our families
Salsi: Burke, Bo, Brian, Jay, Maria, Nathan, and Margaret;
Eubanks: Larry, Mark, Teri, Ashley, Diana, Candace, Barbara, Debbie, and Jo

Surf Bathing, Morehead City, N. C.

CONTENTS

ACKNOWLEDGMENTS

Special thanks to our spouses, Burke Salsi and Larry Eubanks, for their continuing support of our fascination and love of North Carolina history.

We would also like to thank the following: Nettie Murrill, for her love, support, photographs, and memories; Nannie Haley, for her memories, photographs, enthusiasm, and love for the project; Lydia Haley, for her support and friendship; the Carteret County Historical Society and especially to Andrew Duppstadt, executive director, for his continued encouragement; the North Carolina Maritime Museum and for the personal help of Connie Mason, historian. Special thanks go to Connie Mason, for taking the oral history of Mary Snead Dixon while historian for the Cape Lookout National Seashore. We also appreciate the help of Core Sound Waterfowl Museum and for the personal help of Karen Amspacher, executive director; North Carolina Department of Archives and History and for the personal help of Steve Massengill, archivist; the North Carolina Arts in Education Project, based in Greensboro; the Cape Lookout National Seashore, Karen Brown, superintendent, and for the personal help of Karen Dugan, interpretive park ranger; Barbara Gaskin, for sharing her memories; the Outer Banks History Center, Manteo; the Sanitary Restaurant in Morehead City and John Tunnell; Madge Guthrie, Phyllis Gentry, and Jessie Lee Babb Dominique, for sharing their love for Harkers Island, the Banks, and Portsmouth.

All of our information is oral history from the featured participants. A few details were provided by their sons, daughters, brothers, sisters, and brothers. Barbara Garrity Blake's book, *The Fish Factory*, was used for reference. We have not tampered with the "voices," yet we have placed events in chronological order and have edited when necessary to clarify details.

We are grateful for the cooperation from those who shared their stories and their enthusiasm for preserving the history of North Carolina.

INTRODUCTION

This book clearly reflects life in rural Eastern North Carolina at the time of turn-of-the-20th-century innocence and isolation. It contains personal stories of fascinating people who experienced great leaps of North Carolina history. It is a fact, that from its first recorded history until the end of the 1930s, residents of the area experienced a degree of isolation due to the lack of adequate roads. During World War II, it became imperative to protect the coast from German U-boat attacks. Improved roads and rail service came with the establishment of Cherry Point Marine Corp Air Station in Havelock, and this expanded port facilities and coastal fortifications.

World War II forever changed the towns, villages, and hamlets of North Carolina coastal counties. Improved modes of transportation and new roads brought opportunity, and at the same time afforded a "way out" for a generation of young people who sought education and success outside of Carteret County. World War II brought with it a certain eagerness to become part of the outside world.

Unlike most of the coastal communities, the end of the war marked the final blow for the tiny village of Portsmouth. When the Coast Guard withdrew from the Lifesaving Station, no modern conveniences were forthcoming and the community slowly withered.

Today, the structures in Portsmouth Village are on the National Register of Historic Places and are protected by the Cape Lookout National Seashore. The island's history continues to live in the hearts of former residents, descendents, and visitors.

The Crystal Coast of North Carolina is rich in the history and lore of the first settlers in the New World. These "voices" reflect the rich heritage of a past that now only lingers in the memories of a precious few. It is with great satisfaction we present these "voices" so that future generations will know about a special way of life that has been replaced with technological wonders. For certainly without the struggle, dedication, determination, and vision of these valuable coastal families, we would never have come so far.

The Crystal Coast has been so named for the phenomenal beauty of the region. We are pleased to record and share these histories; for without history, there is no future. We hope your reflections on this book will also make you think that your history is important.

—Lynn Salsi and Frances Eubanks
June 2000

Tony Fulcher of Clayton Fulcher Seafood stands by as the crew prepares to off load their catch of the day. Fulcher Seafood is located on the waterfront in Atlantic. (Photo by Frances Eubanks.)

CHAPTER ONE

BEAUFORT
NANNIE VIRGINIA BRANCH HALEY

YOUNG YEARS

I was born a little colored girl in Beaufort, North Carolina. No one could have had a happier childhood.

Beaufort was a small close-knit community. It was the ideal place for a child to grow up. My twin, Evelyn, and I had an older brother, and after we were born, two more sisters came along. My twin sister and I were close. We could walk all over town safely. Not only was the town small, it was bound by water, wilderness, and marsh. Once Cedar Street took the sharp left turn at the top of Live Oak Street, we were out of town— suddenly in the country and a place our parents would not allow us to wander. Nor did we want to go there. We heard stories about the black bears and alligators that might be lying in wait. We were also told about strange and unusual fish and snakes that would be in the murky, swampy waters of creeks, marshes, and rivers.

We always lived close around white people. In the twenties, thirties, and forties, we rarely felt segregated. We were all in it together. It was not an easy time in which to live—low wages and being a million miles from everywhere. Everyone in town knew each other—black and white. When our white postman's daughter needed an operation, my daddy let him have some money to pay for it. If a family was having it hard, everyone pitched in.

Weather played a big part in what we did and where we went. Those were the times that people came to your house and talked about the weather. It was also the time that people understood the weather. They could read signs. There was no television or radio to tell them any different. My mother could tell the time without a watch. She could judge by the sun. She also knew wind direction and not a day went by as long as she lived that she didn't comment on the wind. She'd tell us that the wind talked to her.

As a menhaden fisherman, Bill Branch met the challenges of the sea and worked day and night to provide for his family. He went out on a large boat with 28 men to fish for menhaden, and was away from home for entire months of the year as he travelled to Florida, Delaware, and other places—wherever the fish were running. (Courtesy North Carolina Division of Archives and History.)

She knew the clouds and the feeling of the weather. She could predict storms. My father's work always depended on the weather. She always commented on the conditions and openly worried when he was out during rough weather. Daddy was always glad he wasn't on a boat when the weather was rough.

MENHADEN

Being one of five children meant we had to share. My sisters and I sometimes thought my brother, Bill, had it better than us. He got to go places with the men, and we were told, "It's not for young ladies." My parents and grandparents worked constantly and hard to make ends meet. We never felt poor and we never went hungry. I'm sure that's because they always did their best. In fact, I remember that my family often did for others so that they would not go hungry either.

My father fished on a menhaden boat that carried 28 men. He'd fish in North Carolina in the winter and in Florida in the summer. He also fished in Delaware and New Jersey. Since menhaden had a season, he had to go where the fish were running or stay in Beaufort and do odd jobs between seasons. He chose to have regular pay.

Menhaden crews launched a purse boat and from there they pulled in the fish by hand. They developed a rhythm, from years of working together, that helped them to accomplish the mammoth task. After they raised the net, the fish were hauled into the mother vessel. At the turn of the 20th century through the 1940s, menhaden fishing and processing was a huge industry in Carteret County. (Courtesy North Carolina Division of Archives and History.)

The men lived—ate and slept—on a very large ocean-going boat for days at a time. The work was grueling and back breaking because nets of fish weighing over a ton had to be hauled in by hand—literally. Manpower was required day after day. Daddy had to go off the mother boat and get into a purse boat so he and the other men could get their hands on the huge net. It was a very dangerous profession. My father told stories about the relentless work, the treacherous seas, and how he fell overboard a number of times. He finally retired because the danger was so great.

When he traveled, he'd leave us behind. Beaufort was his and Mama's home. Even when he was not there, we had Mama and our grandparents to watch over us. Daddy faithfully sent money home to us by Western Union so we could live.

We looked forward to Daddy coming home. His homecomings would always be the most exciting times I can remember. He was so loving. He bought the newspaper and read it to us. I loved Flash Gordon. He often said, "I might be dead and gone, but one day a man will walk on the moon."

Lydia Davis Branch was a determined, outspoken woman. She worked full time, took care of her five children, served her church, and loved to dance and sing. Pictured here at the age of 91, she was a lovely lady, small in stature, who liked to look her best. She lived to be 95 years old. (Courtesy Nannie Haley private collection.)

THE FAMILY TREE

My father was my hero. He gave us a good life and expected big things from us. He was good at what he did. He had the reputation for being smart, fair, and interested in his community. He must have been a strong man too, because he was called "the Tiger of the South." One thing is for sure; he worked hard for his money. He worked so hard that we were aware that each year he had to pay a poll tax of $2.00. There was a law stating every male over the age of 21 had to pay the tax. He would say, "Isn't that something, me having to pay for being a man. I can think of a hundred things I could do with that $2.00."

We were all close. My twin sister, Evelyn, and I especially enjoyed each other's company. We were twins, but we didn't look anything alike. She was fair skinned and blond. I am light skinned and brunette and shorter than Evelyn. Daddy told us that we had a lot of different blood running in our veins. That was why we all looked so different. My mother was part Cherokee Indian and my father was white, black, and Cherokee. He was related to the Delamars, a white family that lived in the area.

Everyone in town knew Mother's people. They were the Davis family from the ridge area of Davis Shore, an island in the sound. They originally came to Carteret County as slaves of the Davis family who owned the island. Mother's great-grandfather and his family continued living on the island after the Civil War and came to own part of it. Many

12

Bill Branch was Nannie's father and her hero. He instilled in her the drive to do her best, and worked hard to allow his daughters to become educated. He is shown here holding his grandson, Nannie's youngest child, Bill Haley. (Courtesy Nannie Haley private collection.)

Nannie was named after her aunt, Nannie Virginia Davis Smith. Nannie and her twin, Evelyn, were born two years after this 1923 photo was taken. Shown here are, from left to right, Aunt Nannie's son Johnny, Aunt Nannie (holding Nannie's older brother, Bill, and Nannie's cousin, Mary Ruth), Aunt Gertrude, and Aunt Nannie's son Earl, who grew up to be the director of music at the W.S. King School in Morehead City. (Courtesy Nannie Haley private collection.)

people knew my ancestors because they had lived in the area as far back as anyone could remember. I used to think my Davis kin had always been in Carteret County.

My mother was small and fine in stature but was a powerhouse in spirit. She was always ready to stand up for what was right. She didn't put up with any nonsense. Only one store in Beaufort would let us try on shoes. It was Mr. Sam Lipman's. I remember him telling my mother one time that we weren't allowed to try on shoes. She looked him straight in the eyes and said, "I'm not going to work as hard as I work to pay for these shoes and not have my children try them on." From then on, we shopped there and we tried on our shoes. She was a good

watchful mother and never put up with being cheated. She worked very, very hard and was proud of her children. It was usual for her jobs to last from 6 a.m. to 6 p.m. six days a week for only $3.00 per week.

I learned many valuable lessons from my parents. My father bought me a tablet so I could help keep up with the bills when he was out of town. That way I could go to the store for my mother. Once I went to a local grocery store on Broad Street and picked out a few things my mother needed. I had the grocer write the items on my pad. Then he wrote down two things I didn't get. I said, "No, sir, I didn't get those things. My father taught me that wasn't right." I wouldn't take anything and I walked away. He came after me and then listed the purchase correctly. He always treated me fairly after that. Years later, I went home to visit my parents and I saw that local grocer. He'd remarked about what a smart little girl I'd been.

For awhile Mother worked for various families. Several times she went to Virginia Beach with the Dills to help them while they were on vacation. She only made $3 a week with them. But she did what she had to. That $3 was important to our survival. They had two daughters about our age. Sometimes they would give her clothes or shoes for us. They were nice things that obviously were good quality. The shoes were almost always too narrow.

Mother would look at us and say, "Don't dare say your feet hurt." Those shoes were so narrow it makes my feet hurt now just thinking about it. They hurt, but at least we had shoes.

At one time, Mother worked at the shirt factory in Morehead City. Then during the Depression, she worked at the St. Stephens Church parsonage making pillow cases as part of a Roosevelt WPA program. She didn't stop working until she was 72 years old.

My mother spoke with an accent that I came to appreciate. Hers was a Southern lilt and developed from living in a closed community where people understood each other. She would say, "'deat," instead of "to eat." And when she was mad at me, she would say, "Nannie Virginia Branch!" Other times she would call me "Nan" or "Ginger."

GOOD COOKING

We lived on the corner of Pine and Queen Street. There was a lot to be said about living near the water. We could walk across the street and dip our toes in the river. That was also the place where we put out our crab traps. Daddy would say, "OK, it's time to set our crab traps."

In 30 minutes we could go back and pull up the traps full of crabs. Then we would go home and have the best, freshest crab dinner anyone could ever taste. I learned to clean and stew crabs, although some people fried them first.

My mother and father were both good cooks. They enjoyed good food. There was a lot of pride in my family about serving good food. And throughout my parents' lives, friends and family would comment about my mother's biscuits. Times were hard and I don't know how most people made it, except I never saw anybody go hungry. Back then, people would help one another and share what they had.

We sometimes ate wild rabbit or duck, and when we didn't have fresh fish, we'd eat smoked and salt fish. One time, Daddy caught a big old turtle. He used the big wash pot in the yard to cook it in. Grandmother made delicious little dumplings and threw them into the pot. Turtle was a delicacy, and it was widely enjoyed in the county in the late twenties and thirties.

Whenever we needed a lunch on the go, Mama would pack Gibb's pork and beans and biscuits in a little lunch tin. Those beans were often part of our supper. We'd get mad at our brother Bill because he'd get ahead of us and would sneak one spoonful of beans off of each plate. We also ate a lot of bologna. We'd buy a half a pound or maybe a pound and brown it and make gravy to eat with grits—a lot of grits. When money was scarce, we sometimes ate biscuits and molasses.

Our gardens were always a blessing. We enjoyed fresh vegetables in season. We had collards, shallots, white potatoes, and sweet potatoes. Grandfather had fruit trees, so Mother made fig preserves and pear preserves. She could even make watermelon rind preserves. It was all delicious on warm biscuits—the ones that were talked about in the family and among friends.

Here is my mother's recipe:

2 quarts sifters of plain flour

1 cup of Crisco

2 teaspoons baking powder

1 teaspoon salt

Enough water to mix dough to a smooth consistency

Knead on floured board. Pinch off enough dough for size of biscuit and roll with hands. Place in bread pan and flatten with hand. Bake in 400 degree oven for 15–20 minutes.

My sisters and I had ideas to pick blueberries and sell them. We never made much money because we couldn't help eating them before we got home. Sometimes we had enough left for a pie or blueberry dumplings.

CHILD'S PLAY

As kids, Evelyn, myself, and certain friends liked to run up and down the street going barefoot while wearing long skirts. In the summertime, most of the children were barefooted. I can remember that my shoes were torture to me when I had to put them on for Sunday church.

That was before the street was paved. It was also a time when few people had cars. Beaufort was so out of the way that no one came to town unless they had a reason to come to the county courthouse. June to Labor Day was different; tourist came by train from all over the state and some from up north.

When we were 10 or 12 years old, we would go out and say, "Let's see who is on the train." We enjoyed seeing what the outsiders were wearing. Sometimes the tourists would give us a piece of fruit. Often people would take a sack of fruit when they traveled by train because it was a long and arduous journey even to go to Goldsboro. Sometimes we'd put safety pins on the railroad track; they'd get smashed. We'd gather them after the train passed and use them to make a necklace. We also tried paper clips, but they never worked as well.

We always loved going down to the sound and hanging by our knees on the net spreads. We'd hang upside down and have a good time. When we got tired of that, we'd go down to the water at the edge of the sidewalk and swing our feet out into the sound. It was a carefree thing to do. It's something I remember strongly. At one time, there was also a wonderful beach for colored people at the end of the Lennoxville Road. It was exciting to go on an excursion to Black Cat Beach. There were slides and swings in the water, and Mother would pack a lunch. We'd have a picnic there on the shore. We had just about as much fun as we could stand. Later, someone set fire to the swings and they burned. That was a loss for the children. Today there is an exclusive neighborhood there marked with no trespassing signs.

In warm weather we liked to go to Front Street and sit. We'd watch the tourists out walking and shopping. We'd think of how really rich they must be. We intently studied the way they looked and the way they walked and dressed.

When we were old enough to go around alone, we enjoyed walking all the way across the bridge from Beaufort to Morehead City and on over to Fourteenth and Fisher to a place called Dudley's. It was our big adventure—to go and see what we could see. It was always fun to see what was on the other side. We never got tired of going to see if anything was happening. We weren't the only young people walking back and forth. It was traditional for the Morehead City boys to chase the Beaufort boys and the Beaufort boys to chase the Morehead City boys. Today that couldn't happen because the traffic on the bridge is bumper to bumper. But in the thirties

At the age of six, Nannie was still too small to reach the counter and the table, so her father built a box for her to stand on. Nannie never lost her love for good food and good cooking. She is shown here in her early twenties, in her first apartment in New York City. She has never forgotten her mother's and her father's recipes. (Courtesy Nannie Haley private collection.)

Beaufort was a fish town. Nearly everyone's employment had something to do with the business of fishing. The big fish factory "stunk up" the air and fish houses lined Front Street. Commercial fishing boats were moored close by. Preparing fish was hard, smelly work and paid very little. (Courtesy North Carolina Maritime Museum.)

there were as many people walking across as there were people driving across.

We had an unexpected problem as we matured. We were told any number of times what was appropriate for girls and what wasn't. If we overstepped those boundaries, we were sure to get "the look" from Mother and we felt disapproval from our grandmother and grandfather.

The male members of the family were not shy to mention that girls didn't do certain things. My grandfather had a boat, but he never took the girls anywhere. "They didn't have any business being there" or "it wasn't lady-like." We always

felt that boys had more fun. Owning a boat wasn't a big thing in our family like it was in others. Since Daddy fished for a living, he didn't care about getting in a boat after fishing season was over.

THE FISH BUSINESS

Beaufort was not only a small rural town, it was a fish town. Fishing was what the entire town was about. Nearly everyone's employment had something to do with the water. In the twenties and thirties, fishing was the only thing. The entire shoreline bordering Front Street was lined with fish houses. The menhaden boats pulled into Beaufort to unload the catch. Mullet was also processed and shipped. Barrels of "salt mullet" were a sort of "cash crop." I heard it was an exciting day when the North Carolina and Atlantic Railroad was extended to Beaufort in 1907. The train was known as the "mullet line" and the railroad bridge crossing the channel from Morehead City made it possible for fresh fish and barrels of salted fish to be shipped to all points north, south, and west.

Farmers also depended on rail transportation. Carloads of sweet potatoes and cabbages were shipped. Agriculture was important to the economy, and large farms extended past the city limits. They loaded entire rail cars with bushel baskets full of potatoes and cabbages.

When Harvey Smith put in the big fish factory, it stunk the place up. We smelled fish all the time. It was horrible! When we complained, my father would say, "It smells like money."

One of the fish factories periodically reduced fish for fertilizer. Not only did it smell, it emitted a smog that hung in the air like a heavy veil if there was no breeze.

Daddy would often take us to Front Street. While he transacted or talked to the men, he'd buy us a box of chocolate snaps. We were so content to sit and watch people as we ate our cookies.

We were used to seeing the boats come in and unload their catch at the dock. Men would load a wheelbarrow full of fish and have them for sale right on the street. We could buy a whole string of fish—hogfish, spots, sea mullet for 25¢. When Daddy got off that menhaden boat, he didn't want to have anything to do with fishing. He rarely caught what we ate—someone would share what they had or we'd go and get a string. When I see the price of fish now, I think back to when a quarter sometimes fed our family for more than one meal.

The Blanket Man

It was not unusual to purchase things on time. Mr. Bennett used to go around selling blankets. Those who purchased one from him would pay 25¢ per week until it was paid for. One day we saw Mr. Bennett coming and told Mama that the blanket man was coming.

Mama said, "Tell him I'm not here."

He came on up to the front door and I said, "Mama said to tell you that she's not home because she doesn't have money to give you."

I surely got a whipping for that.

Sunday Church

Our family was particularly religious and attending church was mandatory. My grandfather was a minister at the Holiness Sanctified Church. They had a joyful service playing tambourines and dancing around. During the week he was a fine finish carpenter and cabinet-maker, but his life was his church.

When he got on up in his eighties, he was still preaching. He lived around the corner from his church, yet he would leave home a full hour before he was to preach because he had great difficulty walking. He would walk slowly, very slowly, more like a creeping—around the corner. But when he got inside his church, he found the energy for dancing and going with the spirit.

My father was a faithful church member. We attended St. Stephens Congregational Church, which we considered our home church. We attended there with our mother and father. When we stayed with my grandparents, we attended the church where Grandfather preached.

My twin sister and I loved to sing. In the summer, they put up a platform in front of St. Stephens. My mother, sister, and I got out and sang. Our favorite song was "His Eye Is On the Sparrow." I have a lot of

St. Stephens Congregational Church was the Branch family's home church. Church attendance was mandatory for all of the Branch children. (Photo by Frances Eubanks.)

memories of the music and singing I learned by going to two churches.

My grandfather decided that we were going to be baptized and that he was going to be the one to do it. We went out the West Beaufort Road where the sand bar is, and there we were immersed in water and in the Holy Spirit. He selected this special place instead of the usual waterway straight down Pollock Street. People had gotten down there oystering and had opened so many that there were shells all around. Granddaddy didn't want the discarded shells to cut our feet.

With so much preaching, there was hardly a Sunday that we didn't have a minister in our home for Sunday dinner, which was what is now known as "lunch." We were not allowed to work on Sunday; we were not allowed to even thread a needle. So all the dinner was cooked on Saturday. After church, all we had to do was put the food on the table and eat. Evelyn and I still had to wash dishes.

When the preacher came, it was traditional that he would have the best. For years, I thought the only parts to the chicken were the gizzard, the neck, and the back. This is what the children ate. I thought the rest of the chicken was thrown away. This confused me when I realized Mama had cooked the whole thing. When I saw differently, I asked my father to teach me how to cook.

COOKING CLASS

So when I was six, my father taught me how to cook and how to wash. He was a great teacher. He built me a box to stand on so that I could reach the stove and the table. He taught me how to make biscuits and cook chicken. I had a wonderful time cooking the whole chicken. That's when I learned all the parts. And I can remember how delicious it was to eat a part other than the neck.

He also taught me how to wash clothes and clean up the house. He even showed me how to cut wood and light the stove.

A huge black cast-iron wash pot sat in the yard. It was mainly used for washing and occasionally for cooking turtle soup or a big fish stew. I would help gather and cut the wood and put it underneath the pot for a fire. We boiled clothing in that pot every Monday—wash day.

HOME REMEDIES

We rarely went to the doctor. My parents and grandparents already knew cures for most common ailments. My grandfather grew medicine herbs in his garden along with grapes, figs, and various flowers.

He used cana lilies to help cure headaches. We'd take the petals to the pump and wash them in water and then hold them on our forehead with a clean strip of cloth. For mumps, he'd fry an egg and put turpentine on it. Next he put it in a cloth sack and tied it around the patient's head. When I was about five, I ate it!

Every September, Grandfather would say, "It's cleansing time." Then he would put five drops of linseed oil on granulated sugar. That was our fall cure-all.

Asafetida was used to ward off colds. It was horrible smelling stuff. We'd purchase it at the drugstore, put it in a little sack, and wear it around our necks. It was the accepted help for asthma and coughs. It was also thought to be a preventative medication if used before you were sick. It came in a box from the drugstore.

After we got a cold, a mustard plaster was used. It was made from flour, dry mustard, and water. Grandfather would mix it into a thick paste and rub it on us. As he smoothed it on, he would say, "Shadrach, Meshach, and Abednigo," over and over. It was like a laying on of hands.

At the end of the day, those who worked on the farm received tickets that had to be redeemed at the filling station on Saturday. In the 1930s, everyone worked hard for very little money. Nannie said the work gave the young people something to do, a little money, and kept them out of trouble, and she learned a lot in those fields, including the motivation to study and get an education. (Courtesy North Carolina Division of Archives and History.)

My mother believed in castor oil for a lot of things. Sometimes I thought she was making up all the things that castor oil could cure.

For a cough, she put sugar on a red onion and let it make its own juice. Then she would feed it to us one teaspoon at a time. Honey and lemon were also good for a cough, as was just a tablespoon full of liquor. Vinegar was known to be good for bruises and burns. We'd take strips of brown paper and soak them in vinegar and apply to the wound.

Corn liquor was in everyone's medicine cabinet. It was thought to cure a lot of ails. One thing is for sure; when Prohibition came in, Craven and Carteret Counties were so rural the "corn" business picked up. A lot of people talked about the value of corn and of sugar. The locals knew, however, that it was available when needed. There were a lot of stories about going out Highway 101 and finding "the cure."

Liquor was a valuable ingredient in a lot of our home formulae. When it was put on rock camphor, it made the perfect headache remedy. You could pour a little on your hand or saturate a rag and run it under your nose.

We rarely went to the drugstore. All the old families, black and white, believed in the old cures handed down by grandparents. However, we were lucky to have a drugstore to rely on. Bell's was on Front Street. When we needed something, we'd walk down and stand at a little window on the outside to place our order. It was there just for coloreds. We were not allowed to go in the front door and shop.

ON THE FARM

All the summers of my youth, my sisters and I were hired as laborers to earn extra money to help out. We went to the country, which was down east of Beaufort, and out Highway 101, the original stagecoach road from Havelock to Beaufort. Mama protected us from the sun by dressing us in old shirts and sun hats. We worked in the fields picking beans, white potatoes, and other vegetables.

I walked behind the horse that was attached to a plow. As the plow loosened the earth, I would pick the potatoes up and put them into a bushel basket. Sometimes I would have to pull them from the ground and shake off the dirt. When the basket was full, a man would come, take it, and give me another empty.

We were only paid 3¢ a bushel. About the time I was nine or ten, I set out sweet potato plants using a two-pronged stick and chopped tomato plants for $1.25 a day. At the end of the day, we received tickets that had to be redeemed at the filling station on Saturday. Once the man cashing in the tickets told my mother that we were getting too much money. She got really mad. She picked up a pail and threatened to throttle him, saying, "I'm not taking my children out in the hot sun to work like that and not get paid what we are owed." Nobody, but nobody, was going to cheat my mother for all of her hard work.

We didn't mind going out picking beans and potatoes. It gave us something to do and Mama knew where we were. We contributed to our family, yet we could keep a little money for our own entertainment. Working on the farm kept a lot of children out of trouble. It probably also helped to convince a lot of young people to get out of Beaufort because they didn't want to fish and pick vegetables for the rest of their lives. I liked having a little money and I liked to socialize. I can still remember when I was old enough to flirt with the boys. When I think about it, I also remember my mother saying that I was smiling too much and being too friendly.

The fields we worked were across the street from a place where old people who had no where to go and no money were sent. It was a sad sight to see those

The Branch children worked on a farm in the country near the "poor house"—the Carteret County Home. The Carteret County Home has been renovated and is now a charming bed and breakfast on Highway 101. (Photo by Frances Eubanks.)

hopeless old people. The place was the county home, but it was called "the poor house." At least that is what everyone in Beaufort called it. My grandmother was always telling us to handle our money wisely. She'd say, "Handle your money wisely or you'll end up in the poor house." That made a big impression on all of the children. We certainly didn't want to end up there.

The building is still there on Highway 101. Someone has renovated it and made it into a bed and breakfast. It is still called the county home.

NOTHING FOR NOTHING

Children in the twenties and thirties didn't get handouts of money or candy. We never got nothing for nothing.

The children in our family were always taught to work. If we wanted to buy a stick of candy or see a movie or get a Pepsi, we had to earn the money. We would go over to the fish house and work our fingers to the bone opening scallops just to earn 50¢. That's all that anybody made for doing the job.

But 50¢ would buy a lot. I liked to drop in at the Quick Lunch and buy a "dried chicken" (like a honey bun) and a Pepsi. If we felt like we were in the "chips," we'd buy a bologna sandwich for a nickel and a Pepsi for a nickel.

CHRISTMAS

Christmas was a special time. We were excited to get out of school for the holidays. There were special services at

When working in the fields, Nannie walked behind a horse that was attached to a plow. She picked up potatoes and put them into a bushel basket. Produce was shipped to other parts of the state by the North Carolina and Atlantic Railroad, which came right down Ann Street. (Courtesy North Carolina Division of Archives and History.)

church and lots of pies and cakes. Sometimes churches would fill round bushel baskets with groceries and give them out. We enjoyed receiving a basket.

There would be a special Christmas parade and a group of men would dress up like Santa Claus. I remember Walter Joyner dressing up. The men would parade up and down the street inviting everyone, "Come out! Come out!" Sometimes they would run up on people's porches calling, "Come out!" The people might run into their houses and lock the door if they spotted the Santas coming their way. It was all done in fun.

Santa Claus visited our house, and his coming created a great deal of excitement. On Christmas Eve, we were careful to go to bed early. I remember when I didn't know the truth about Santa Claus. One Christmas, I peeked behind a chest of drawers and saw a doll. That did it! I knew about Santa then. Mother wasn't happy when she found out, but she gave me the doll anyway.

WORLD WAR II

When World War II began, we knew things were quite serious on our coast. We could actually see and hear bombings. We heard a lot about bodies washing up on the beach. We saw airplanes going over all the time. Every time I'd look up and think, "I sure hope that's ours."

The war was talked about on the street and over the dinner table. I was in my next to last year of high school. Many of the young men I knew were gung-ho to join up. My brother Bill had joined the Navy in

Nannie's twin sister's husband, Guy Copes, served in the Army during World War II. Aside from day-to-day rationing, Carteret County residents could hear U-Boat torpedoes as they struck American ships. (Courtesy Nannie Haley private collection.)

1939, and when the war started, we were concerned about his safety. There was a certain anxiety among the adults. It couldn't help being felt by all the children. It was an awful feeling. We sometimes had a feeling of doom.

There were no streetlights and shades had to be pulled down in all of the windows at night. Everyone attached a piece of black paper half way over the headlights so they would not shine brightly. The idea was to conceal as much light as possible so the coast would not be outlined for the Germans to see. Black-outs were required all up and down the coast.

All the time the enemy was right out there nearby. We knew they were there

and we felt their presence even though we could not see them. It was surprising they could get that close to our shore.

COURTING

My father always said that he had a gun polished up for the man that wanted to marry Nannie. I liked talking to the boys because that was about all anyone could afford. My mother thought differently. She'd see me smiling and talking to the boys. I thought it was fun. She'd say over and over, "You're going to end up with a room full of children." I'd tell her I wasn't going to do anything that I wasn't supposed to do. I was just having fun.

Between the Depression and the war, no one had any money. That limited our choices of entertainment when we were courting. We could go to a movie in town on Front Street, go for a walk, go to church, or hang out around the house. If a boy walked me home after dark, we might stand at the edge of our front yard fence and talk awhile. My father would come out and say, "OK, I don't want my daughter hanging on the fence and in the corners. Come on in the house."

Sometimes we'd take our courting in the house and sit in the living room. The couch was behind the door. When Mother was sitting in a chair in her bedroom next to the living room, we'd start talking and she'd answer from the other room.

We might sit in the swing on the porch. My parents' bed was right by the open window. If we walked off the porch so that we could have a little privacy, Daddy would get up and yell out, "Stop hanging on the fence and get out of the corners."

He really worked at keeping the boys away from his daughters. He'd say, "Look, my girls are going to finish school," or he'd say, "My girls aren't having any company because they have to get an education."

One day I was supposed to be cleaning the kerosene lamp chimneys. They were black and sooty and it was always a chore to clean them. It was pointless to light the lamps if the chimneys were black. This certain day, Bill Horton came by to talk to me. I put my work aside and lost track of the time talking to him. My daddy came in and was so mad that I'd not done my chores that Bill ran off and forgot his cap. I got a whipping because I had not done my chores. We knew that if we were told to do something we'd better do it.

Going to see a movie was a big deal. It was the best entertainment available. On Saturday when I could earn enough extra money, I'd go with friends and my sister. We saw a lot of Westerns and I particularly remember "Alexander's Ragtime Band." In those days I wondered what it must be like to sit in front of the screen on the first level of the theater. We were colored and we had to walk up three sets of stairs to the balcony. We were required to sit there.

SCHOOL DAYS

I went to Queen Street High School, where I got a good education. Those were the days when we started every day with the Pledge of Allegiance to the flag and had a prayer. Those were also the days that students behaved or else.

The principal, Mr. Best, was very strict. He always knew what was going on. He would spank the girls and boys if they misbehaved. Then he would call the parents and the kids would get whipped again.

I was 16 when I graduated from high school after the 11th grade. Schools then only had 11 grades. When Evelyn and I were little, my mother had to work, and she was worried about how to care for us. She decided to enroll us in school at the age of five instead of the mandatory age of

Here is a rare photograph of all the Branch girls together. From left to right are Dorothy, Evelyn (Nannie's twin), Mrs. Lydia Branch, Nannie, and Katy. They were all together attending a relative's wedding. (Courtesy Nannie Haley private collection.)

six. She went down and enrolled us in first grade and told the school we were six. And then she told us we were six. She said, "Don't you tell or you know what's coming."

We enjoyed school activities. My twin, Evelyn, was tall enough to play basketball. I sang in the Glee Club. We were not allowed to sing unless we could recite the words of our songs perfectly. On May Day each year, we danced around the Maypole.

I had a real problem with math. I couldn't understand my lessons. I got to the point I didn't like it, so I went to Daddy. My father taught me so much. One night at dinner I told him I was in trouble with physics. He went only to the fourth

This photo was taken at Nannie's younger sister Dorothy's wedding to James McIntyre. From left to right are the following: Dorothy's mother-in-law, Mrs. McIntyre; Dorothy; James McIntyre; Mrs. Lydia Branch; and Guy Copes, who is Nannie's nephew and is now the director of the housing authority. (Courtesy Nannie Haley private collection.)

grade but was good with figures. He took the time to explain my lessons to me. I breezed through after that.

Years later when I was in New York working at the stock exchange, I thought about my father often and how he had helped me. I worked with the daily stock record and had to clear the records by 3 o'clock. I started working with the Depository Trust Company when they were in just one room.

Electricity Comes

Our time was controlled by daylight until I was almost out of high school. And then we got electricity. It was almost 1937 when we got power. Many others in town had it before we did, but my parents were not convinced that it was a good thing. After all, we had gotten along without it. Most nights I studied and read books by a kerosene lamp. I remember struggling through reading books and then writing book reports in dim light. I could easily tell the difference after we got electricity. It was brighter than kerosene. Actually, I was thrilled not to have to trim wicks and clean lamp chimneys.

The best thing about electricity was that we could have a radio. I remember being thrilled to have a radio. It was the first time the outside world came into our lives on a daily basis. My daddy loved to hear Western music. We'd sit in front of the radio and listen with him.

This is what Fisher Street in Morehead City looked like in the 1920s and early 1930s. Nannie and Evelyn enjoyed the long walk across the bridge to Morehead City so that they could go to Dudley's on Fisher Street and drink a Pepsi and listen to the juke box. (Courtesy Salsi/Eubanks private collection.)

TEEN YEARS

At 15 and 16, Evelyn and I loved to dance. My mother was careful where she allowed us to go. There was a place on Queen Street called the Quick Lunch, where we could dance. She would walk us over, let us go in, and we could dance for 15 minutes. Mama would stay outside and sit on a neighbor's steps while waiting for us.

We stood a good chance of going to the Quick Lunch if we went to church. Our reward might be getting a Pepsi for a nickel and a bologna sandwich for a nickel.

I remember one of the trips Evelyn and I made to Morehead City. We went on a date; Rudolph Sparrow was one of the boys. We went to Dudley's on Fisher Street to play the jukebox and drink a Coke. Mother had just bought Evelyn and I a new pair of shoes—we were feeling dressed up. Afterwards, the boys got a little fresh with us and we got mad so they refused to take us home. They put us out of the car right where the bridge crosses the channel. We were stuck in Morehead City facing a long walk home in the dark.

As we got out, Evelyn lost one of her shoes. We were certainly facing a dilemma. We had a long walk home and Evelyn had only one shoe. We sat down on a bench near the port talking about what we could do. Mother would be mad if she found out we had to walk home after dark and she'd really be mad when we told her that Evelyn had lost a brand-new shoe.

We were delaying the inevitable when my Uncle Dan, who owned the local taxi service, drove by and saw us. He took us

Nannie's younger sister Katy poses on the steps of their house at 504 Pollock Street. (Courtesy Nannie Haley private collection.)

Nannie poses in her prom dress in front of the Branch house. (Courtesy Nannie Haley private collection.)

home lecturing us all the way. But he did promise not to tell on us.

We decided that I should take off my shoes and we'd walk in the house barefooted. Mother noticed and wanted to know why we didn't have shoes on. We told her since they were new, they were pinching a little. We walked straight to our room and prayed real hard that night that Rudolph would bring the shoe. He came through for us. The next morning he showed up with Evelyn's shoe. I've remembered him favorably ever since.

Mother was sure that we were going to be protected. When we went on a date, she would walk out and stand in the middle of the street to be sure that we were headed in the right direction. We'd say, "Mother, we're going to see a movie." She'd stand in the street and watch us as far as she could watch just to make sure we were going toward Front Street.

MAN OF MY DREAMS

In 1940 Evelyn and I were enjoying a Sunday walk after church. As usual, we were going over to Morehead City. When we got across the bridge, we saw a Coast Guard cutter, the *Pamlico*, at the port dock. So we headed over to see what was going on. When we got closer, we noticed that the flag was flying upside down. We heard, "Hey, Haley, you've got the flag upside down."

When Nannie met Alex Haley, he was in the Coast Guard serving on the Pamlico, *a cutter. He was stationed in New Bern, but the boat was docked at the port in Morehead City. (Courtesy Nannie Haley private collection.)*

We stopped right beside the cutter and Alex Haley came on deck to take care of the flag. He looked over the side and saw us staring. He looked right at me and said, "What's your name?"

That was our first meeting, but he must have remembered me. Several weeks later I went to the Quick Lunch and there he was dancing with a girl he may have been dating. We said, "Hello," and because Mother only let me stay 15 minutes, I left.

Evelyn and I asked my mother to take us to New Bern to attend a dance. In the late thirties and forties, there were many big dances in New Bern featuring well-known orchestras like Lionel Hampton. Actually we didn't have to beg too hard to go because Mother enjoyed good music and she also liked to dance. It was her policy that we weren't going 35 miles away without her. Mother had a friend with a car and we all went to New Bern. We were thrilled to take any trip out of town. When we got there, I couldn't believe it; that good-looking Coast Guard man was there. Alex Haley was at the dance. He recognized me and came over and said, "Hello, I'll bet you don't remember my name."

That began our courtship and we fell in love. Alex often called the radio station and requested our special songs: "The Very Thought of You," "String of Pearls," and "Stardust." He had them dedicated to Nan.

Mrs. Alex Haley was in her early twenties when this photograph was taken. She was married during World War II—not long before Alex was shipped out. She went home to live with her parents until Alex returned from overseas duty. (Courtesy Nannie Haley private collection.)

I was 17 and my father thought Alex Haley was "too fast" for me. Actually, he didn't want me to date a sailor. That was his opinion and that was all he had to say. But I was in love and I was getting married.

By then the war had started. Alex's cutter, the *Pamlico*, was stationed in New Bern. He knew he was about to go on maneuvers, so while "Star Dust" was playing on the jukebox, Alex Haley proposed and asked me to come to New Bern to marry him.

I told my mother I was going to get married. She didn't say much. I guess she accepted the inevitable. I got a ticket and caught a Trailways Bus to New Bern. My twin, Evelyn, had already married and was not able to go with me. So, I went alone. Alex met me at the foot of the bridge that crosses the Neuse River. The *Pamlico* was moored nearby, so when I arrived all the sailors were out on the deck to get a good look at the girl Haley was marrying. We were married by a local minister on August 21, 1942.

During much of the war, Alex was stationed overseas. I moved back to Beaufort to live at home with my parents. I waited for his return and for the birth of our first child.

Lydia Anne Haley was the first black baby born in the Morehead City Hospital. Doctor Hyde delivered her. Afterward, I was sent to a room in the basement. At that time, that was where the black patients had to go. My hospital bill was only $30 for ten days.

I think my twin sister's husband's grandmother was mad at me for choosing the hospital. A well-known midwife, she had delivered everybody's baby in the area and was something of a character. She was a really tiny woman and wore white all the time. Her long skirt was topped with an apron. I was present when she delivered my sister's baby at home. I knew right then that when I had children I wanted a doctor and a hospital.

Lydia Anne Haley was the first black baby born in Morehead City Hospital. (Courtesy Nannie Haley private collection.)

She was put out with me that I didn't want her to deliver my baby. But when growing up, I had been told that babies came from stumps in the woods. I spent a lot of time crying on rainy nights worrying about those poor babies getting wet under stumps. It was definite—a doctor and ten days in a hospital.

Lydia Anne was almost two years old before Alex came home in 1944. He was stationed in New York and wanted us to join him. By then, North Carolina had passenger train service to New York. Daddy had his brother, my Uncle Dan, take me to Rocky Mount to catch the train. Before I left, my father and I had a special talk. He said, "Remember, you are leaving home to better yourself. You never worked in a kitchen or kept

Nannie Haley is pictured here at a presentation for the Carteret County Historical Society in Morehead City. (Photo by Frances Eubanks.)

EDITOR'S NOTE

Nannie Haley was ahead of her time; she was a career woman in the 1940s. She grew up in a very small, closed community with very few worldly influences and yet was able to move to New York City and succeed. In fact, Nannie succeeded past her wildest dreams. She experienced the rise of her own success and also that of her husband, Alex Haley. She always carried something with her for Alex to write on. Yet this is the story of her young life—the story of growing up with family and friends. The story of *Roots* is another one altogether.

Nannie's voice adds to the aura and charm of Beaufort, famous for its place in colonial history. Her history is interwoven with the people who lived there in the 1930s and 1940s. Nannie and her daughter, Lydia Anne, have been a part of a very special "lunch bunch." I always wanted to be "one of the ladies who lunch," so now when I'm in town, lunching with the Haley girls is a "must." Nannie and Lydia make you want to take the time to smell the roses.

—Lynn Salsi

anyone's children. So don't go up there doing any of that."

So, I left my family and went to New York City. It was such an adventure; I had never been out of Carteret County. I was a young modern woman. I worked at the stock exchange and was a wife and mother. Alex attended his Coast Guard duties and wrote every chance he got. I can remember the excitement every time he sold a story to a magazine. That little bit of extra money was very important. We called those checks "pot-boilers" because it meant we could eat a little better. He never stopped writing and I never stopped working so he could write. And the rest is history.

CHAPTER TWO

MOREHEAD CITY
NETTIE WILLIS MURRILL

WE HAD IT ALL

Morehead City may as well have been the center of the universe, at least as far as I was concerned. We had it all—enough food to eat, a roof over our heads, and the train arriving and departing, one a day, right through the middle of Arendell Street. There was never another place like Morehead and the Promise Land. We could fish and pick up clams and play in the water everyday.

When I was born in 1911, Morehead City was considered to be in the "middle of nowhere." It was rural. And I knew it was. Everybody knew everybody and if someone new came to town, everybody knew it. The town was built on what used to be Shepard Point. It was established in 1857 by John Motley Morehead, the former governor, and his crowd. He was intent on establishing a port and routing a railroad to it. He accomplished all three objectives. Lots were sold, the railroad was built, and a port was constructed right

on Beaufort Inlet and Bogue Sound. Everything is still there today like he envisioned it.

Morehead City was a small town until World War II. There was just a strip of a business area with shops on each side of the road. The railroad tracks were laid right down the middle of Arendell Street with the train depot at the end. This left enough land so that it could become the wide boulevard it is today. I have a photograph taken from an airplane in 1938. You can see how sparsely populated the town was. Yet life in Morehead City was pleasant. People greeted each other. They sat on their front porches and if people were in need, they helped their neighbors.

EARLY ROADS

At first, all of the roads and streets were hard-packed dirt covered with shells. We called them shell roads. The shell road

In 1917 the train depot was in the middle of Arendell Street. Morton's Store was in the large building in the foreground. Dr. Ben Royal, Nettie's distant cousin, started the first hospital in Morehead City, occupying half of the top floor. He later took over the entire second floor before building a hospital on the waterfront. (Courtesy Eubanks/Salsi private collection.)

Arendell Street was paved in 1927 and resembled a thoroughfare. The street was paved on both sides of the railroad track. Except for parallel parking, it still retains the same look. (Courtesy Eubanks/Salsi private collection.)

The New Roads Association was established to help improve roads across North Carolina that would ultimately connect Mountain City, Tennessee, to Morehead City via Highway 70. This Scout Car made the trip along the route in August 1913. Political maneuvering was involved in having the road come to Morehead City instead of Beaufort. The purpose of the movement was to connect rural communities to the rest of the state as a way of helping with the transportation of agricultural products. (Courtesy Eubanks/Salsi private collection.)

went as far as the Bayview Cemetery. As it wore down, more shells would be added. When there was a funeral, we'd run ahead of the hearse to tell Lev Garner, the official gravedigger, "They're coming! They're coming!"

Lev knew all about graves. He knew the size, the depth, and dug all the graves by himself with one shovel. His graves were dug perfectly with sides straight up and down. When the person was buried, he would fill it in and fashion a mound on top. I can remember him patting the top gently with his hands. He was a very proud man.

The Bayview Cemetery wasn't so far from our house that we couldn't occasionally have an adventure. Mamie, Sadie, and I would go over and talk to Lev. He'd be digging a grave and would let us climb down into it. Once, my sister Mamie got in and we had the darndest time

getting her out. Lev went and got something for her to stand on so she could climb out.

Lev passed away and Mr. Lewis took over the grave digging. By then I was too old to run down the road.

Our streets and roads were not paved until 1927. Of course, it didn't much matter because few people had a car. They probably couldn't have afforded one, yet they didn't need one. There was no bridge to or from Morehead City to Beaufort until 1928, so everyone needed a boat. That was the main mode of transportation.

When the roads were paved, it was pretty exciting and I remember thinking we were getting somewhere. Of course, Highway 70 was about the only road that got paved. It was part of a government program for improving roads. Once you were two blocks to the north of Arendell

Nettie remembered passing the Pigott farmhouse when she went by wagon to visit the farms on Crab Point across Calico Creek. Emeline Pigott was a famous Civil War spy. Confederate soldiers camped on the Pigott land. This is a photo of the house taken in the 1940s as it fell into disrepair. The farm later became the site of a housing development. (Aycock Brown photograph; courtesy North Carolina Division of Archives and History.)

Street, there was nothing but dirt streets. We called that the country. Once we passed the Bayview Cemetery and crossed the bridge over Calico Creek, we were in the country where there was nothing but farms. To go that 3 or 4 miles by horse and cart was a major undertaking.

Poppy sometimes traded barrels of salt mullet, fresh fish, oysters, and scallops to farmers across the creek. He could trade one barrel of salted mullet for four or five barrels of cracked corn. Once or twice my mother hired a horse and cart and driver and took my sisters and me to the farm to visit for the day. We got up early, packed a lunch, put our hats on, and had the best time sitting up in the cart. When we got across the rickety little bridge across the creek, a boy had to come and let us through the gate. Cattle roamed over the land and the gate was at the bridge to keep them from walking off the property.

We got a lot of fresh vegetables and then went home. We worked like dogs to preserve them.

A GOOD LIFE

Life was good between 1911 and 1929. My father, Gilbert Willis, I called him Poppy, had a regular job. In a time when most of the population had to fend for themselves, he was so lucky. He was a captain and a caretaker for Mr. John Motley Morehead II, who was the grandson of the founder of Morehead City. After the elder Morehead's death, Poppy worked for his son, Mr. Lindsay Morehead. When he was not captaining for the Moreheads, he was looking after their property on Arendell Street. He also took them and guests fishing, and worked as their hunting guide.

Nettie's father was considered the best sailor in Morehead City. For years he won almost all of the sailboat races. Nettie's father, or Poppy, let his girls sail with him to Beaufort. Nettie's job was to handle the jib. She related what a thrill it was to cross the channel just to see what the people on the other side looked like. (Courtesy Nettie Murrill private collection.)

The Morehead boat was moored at the Morehead City waterfront near where the Sanitary Restaurant is today. Through the years, they owned three boats. Nettie especially remembered the Reliance. *This is a scene of the waterfront in the 1920s. In the foreground is a net reel for commercial fishing nets. Most commercial boats were moored at the waterfront. (Courtesy Eubanks/Salsi private collection.)*

He was lucky to have a regular job for nearly 30 years. He got the job because he was with a captain working as a mate. They took the Morehead family out, and Mr. John Motley Morehead asked the captain to come work for him. He said, "No, I've got a job here, Mr. Morehead. But Gib here, doesn't have a regular job and he's getting married." When they returned to the mainland, Poppy was in Mr. Morehead's employ and was as long as the family vacationed in Morehead City. Poppy earned $100 a month, which was decent pay.

My mother, Hannah Guthrie Willis—I called her Mommy—was a housewife. She kept the cleanest house in the neighborhood, raised her girls, and took in sewing to help make ends meet.

My Poppy did everything well. He wasn't a boatbuilder like our cousin, Julian Guthrie, but he knew everything about boats. He had a vast knowledge of sailing and had experience as the master of all kinds of boats. It was amazing how he could have the sails out, bring the boat to a dead stop, and then sail backwards. He understood wind direction and was also an expert weatherman.

I loved sailing with Poppy. I remember sitting and handling the jib. I got real good at it. He wouldn't let us sail by ourselves. We had to man the centerboard or the jib. It was a great honor to throw the anchor out. He cut his own sails and Mommy helped him sew them. I still have his "pam" (palm) somewhere. He'd say, "You can't put the sails you want on a boat. You have to put on the sails that suit the boat." He taught us how to hold on if the skiff ever turned over. Right before he died, he admitted that he had never learned to swim but that he had a cork life preserver under his seat.

One thing's for sure; Poppy never challenged Mother Nature. He had better sense than to ever be caught out in bad weather. He could read all the signs—he could read the weather. He'd say, "Look and see if the sky is red this evening. If so, we can go wherever we plan tomorrow."

Poppy taught us the Bible verse Matthew 16: 1–3, and it is something I've never forgotten.

1. The Pharisees and Sadducees came to Jesus and tested him by asking him to show them a sign from heaven.
2. He replied, "When evening comes, you say, 'It will be fair weather, for the sky is red,'
3. and in the morning, 'Today it will be stormy, for the sky is red and overcast.' You know how to interpret the appearance of the sky, but you cannot interpret the signs of the times.

We didn't have a car and didn't need one. All of the places we went required a boat, not a car. We had to take a boat to reach Beaufort and the little towns Down East. Poppy always said he wouldn't have a car if you gave him one. He and we walked everywhere. He walked back and forth everyday from our house near Shackleford and Thirteenth Street down to Fourth Street and Arendell, where the Morehead summerhouse was located. Some days he would walk the distance many times. He might have to come home to get a hammer or his push lawnmower, or he might have to detour to the waterfront to work on one of the Morehead boats. Their boats were tied up about where the Sanitary Restaurant is today.

We mostly measured wealth by whether a family had an automobile or not. In the twenties people who had money started having second homes in Morehead City. We called them "cottagers." Since we didn't have much in common with them, we didn't mingle. The Moreheads definitely fit into the monied category. They had two cars—both Packard Town Sedans. Poppy said they needed cars but we didn't because we had a boat.

There was never much discussion about people being rich or poor. It wasn't hard to figure out that the outsiders were wealthy. Poppy would say, "That's what it's like to be rich."

THE PLACE TO BE

In the summertime the world came to us. Vacationers came to the Atlantic Hotel, which was a famous resort. It was so large it covered a city block and had a ballroom as big as a football field.

Even the Governor of North Carolina came. His yacht would be tied up at the hospital dock. The train delivered and picked up vacationers. The hotel was only a few blocks from our house on Shackleford Street. We could walk down and see the hotel guests strolling the docks and bathing in the sound. As a young teen, I'd get in a group and go out on the dock in the evening. We'd pretend that we were staying at the hotel. We'd sit, talk, and hold our heads just so, pretending that we were worldly and sophisticated.

Swimming was unheard of. People enjoyed the water—wading and bathing. The word "swimming" was not in our vocabulary; we said "going in bathing." The hotel guests had special bathing suits.

My sisters and I loved to go bathing in the sound. We put on our oldest dresses and drawers and waded in the water. On hot summer days we'd squat down and

This photograph of Nettie's mother was taken on a sandy shoal behind the houses on Shackleford Street in Morehead City. (Courtesy Nettie Murrill private collection.)

giggle as we watched our skirts billow out over the water. We didn't go in any farther than knee deep. Sometimes we would paddle around a little.

DAY ONE

All of the families in town were like ours. They had descendents who had lived somewhere in Carteret County for over a hundred years, sometimes for two hundred. I knew that our people had been in North Carolina from day one, even though Poppy and Mommy didn't know where the first Willis and the first Guthrie had come from. I thought everybody's family was like ours. They had all been there as far back as anyone could remember. They all had names like Guthrie, Willis, and Mason. My mother had been a Guthrie who married a Willis.

Many of the Willises and Guthries had intermarried with a few other families so many times that I had a "blue million" cousins. I was just reading a book of family histories recently and found out that Ellen Cloud is a distant cousin. I've known her for years and just realized that she was a cousin.

Morehead City didn't get on the map until the time of the Civil War, but Beaufort had a history that dated back to the early 1700s. It was a destination for vacationers in the 1800s. I have memories of people in Beaufort thinking they were really more important than the people in Morehead. I guess they just looked at the Morehead settlers as upstarts since Morehead wasn't established until 1857.

PRACTICAL UPBRINGING

I had a very practical upbringing. Both of my parents had ancestors who had been hardworking people who were self-sufficient. They had been taught to make the most of what they had. They passed these lessons on to my sisters and me. We had to learn to take care of ourselves. Then later, we would know how to take care of our families.

This was in the second decade of the twentieth century. It was the time women were slaves to work in their own homes. Someone had to do it. My parents had four daughters, and we were assigned to many tasks.

We had to learn to carry out our chores, and we were expected to do them without being told but once. Efficiency was the "word" to describe my mother's and father's teaching technique.

My sisters and I became first-class domesticated ladies. My family was of moderate means and not of the income to hire help unless it was an emergency. Even then most of the people who were available to help lived on one of the farms outside of town.

Uncle Kib's store was down the street from the Willis house. The store had a famous structural problem—it leaned. It was something of a wonder because everyone thought it might fall down at any time. Nettie's father and other men from the community would gather at the store to talk about the weather and where the fish were biting. (Courtesy Madge Guthrie private collection.)

My mother was strict with us about everything and she never let us run around without her knowing what we were doing and where we were going. That included the way we carried out all of our chores. She taught us an exact way to hang up the laundry and how to bring it inside. We had to fold and bring things in properly. The big items like sheets were taken down first. They were folded on the line by pulling one side of the sheet over, unpinning the clothespin. Then bringing the bottom up from the top, taking the rest of the pins out, and folding again. Next came the pillowcases and then the pants, dresses, and shirts. If they were starched, they had to be ironed. If they were not starched, they could be smoothed out and we would not have to iron. Since we had no closets, newly dried and folded items were placed in the chest of drawers—neatly.

After putting the clean things away, we counted the clothespins. If there were any missing, we had to go back out and search until we found the missing ones.

As a child, all of my days were on a set schedule—everyday was cut out.

On Mondays, we had to wash clothes, hang them on the line, and take them in when they were dry. If it rained, we did chores for another day on that day. If it rained more than two days in a row, it wrecked the plans for the week. Washing was all by hand in a big pot outside. A scrub board was a valuable piece of equipment (I still have one). Elbow grease was also important because the scrubbing was what got the clothes clean.

Tuesday was ironing day. I felt sorry for my mother. With four girls, she had more than her share of ironing. Wednesday was the day for mending and sewing. Friday was the day for baking. Mommy let us stir things a little but we were nearly grown before she let us cook and bake without her help. She had a fear of us getting burned on her old cook stove.

Saturday was the day for cleaning. Mommy had "this clean thing." We mopped the kitchen with an old towel or a great big rag. It was also the children's job to wash the porch; we washed that back porch to death. Since it dried from the breeze, heat, or sun, the deed had to be carried out early in the day so it would not rot. Our porches were so clean we could lie on them. After supper we'd go out and lie on the porch. Mommy would tell us tales. I don't think she ever finished one but that's what kept us wanting her to tell us. She'd say, "This really happened." We'd say, "Mommy, tell it!"

I always thought that our porch must be the cleanest. Mommy wanted everything cleaned and recleaned just in case someone came to see us. They'd say, "Hannah's porch is the cleanest I ever saw." If someone ever commented on what a good housekeeper she was, it would make her even more "gung-ho" about cleaning.

That clean porch became the perfect place to stage our shows. Every now and then my sisters and I would think it might be fun. We invited all the children we knew to come to our house to see the show. Admission was one safety pin, which was not a small price. They were hard to come by and we used those pins.

I was probably 10 or 11. Alma was only five but she and Sadie sang a duet. Then we said things we had learned in school. We all danced a little like a soft shoe we had seen in a movie. We had seen a lot of Westerns at the picture show which had girls dancing in barroom scenes. We tried

a little of that too. Our favorite costume was to find some women's hats and pretend that we were adults.

On Saturday after chores, I liked to walk down to Uncle Kib Guthrie's store that was only a block from our house. It was a gathering place for everyone. It was "the place" to go in our neighborhood. I could get cheddar cheese tidbits for 5¢ and a giant dill pickle for 5¢. Those pickles were a special treat—big, sour, and crunchy. I'd go with my sisters and all the other little girls in the neighborhood.

I can close my eyes now and see us walking down Shackleford Street hand in hand giggling and talking. I can see the men who might gather for a little while to talk about the weather, fishing, and where the best fishing ground might be. I remember going with Poppy to get groceries. The men would stop him and ask, "Gib, where're you catching fish?"

He'd stop, squat down, and draw a map in the dirt with a stick. He'd say, "We were coming along by Marshy Point east of Crab Point near the Haystacks. It was the first time I ever saw so many mullet coming through the Haystacks." After Poppy got old, Kib's store was where he and his friends would sit and talk about the old days and always about fishing.

A WORLD OF WORK

We had a good and happy life but everyone had to pull their weight, even the children. Parents didn't give children money. When they got old enough, they hired themselves out to the neighbors who needed help to do the same stuff they had already learned to do at home. Talk about child labor; I remember working for a neighbor lady straightening up, dusting, and washing dishes for 50¢ per week. I also ran errands, cleaned house, and brought clothes in off the line. Fifty cents was certainly not much, but at the time that was all it was worth for those who were paying.

Mommy and Poppy didn't have the opportunity to go to school. In the late 1800s public schools were open only three or four months of the year. It was more important that the young males learned about how to make a living and practical things like that—surviving. School was never in session during fishing season. It was very important to my parents that my sisters and I get an education.

During the Depression, the WPA paid teachers to teach simple education to people who had lacked schooling. My mother learned to write and was proud when she could sign her name. I can remember how proud she was when she could read.

Since my father didn't read or write, I remember that when I was in the sixth grade, I became his secretary. I always enjoyed writing his letters. That's probably what inspired me to go to business college when I graduated from high school.

Mr. Morehead called him "Skipper." His letters would say:

Dear Skipper:
Mr. Morehead asked me to have you get certain supplies.

It would be signed by Blanche Choate, his secretary.

I would read Mr. Morehead's letters to Poppy and then write his orders. I wrote to the National Net and Twine Company and said:

Dear Sir:
Enclosed you will find my check for so many pounds of cotton net advertised on page 34 in your recent catalogue.
Yours very truly,
Captain Gilbert Willis

I've seen my father take the net and fasten it to rope. He'd get it real tight. Then he'd throw it around and be sure it was right. He would then fasten the lead making a lead line. The space in the net

called the "marsh" but spelled "mesh" determined the type of fish that could be caught.

Mommy could weave a net from twine. It was knowledge that was handed down through generations. Nets were the most valuable tool of fishing families. She would knit the netting on a wooden fid. The fid was fastened to twine. It was fascinating to watch. After using the nets, Poppy would hang them to dry on net spreads he built at the edge of the water.

When I was 12, I'd go down to one of the fish houses and help open scallops. We thought it was good money yet we had to work our fingers off to get 10¢. I needed the money to buy myself a piece of candy, cookies, or admission to the picture show.

During my entire childhood, I helped my mother in the house and helped my father pull weeds in the garden. I went fishing and clamming with him. I could do it blind-folded. We loved going floundering at night. The man of the house was the one to gig the flounder.

FISHING

Fishing was a big deal for all the men in the community. In fact, it was the only deal. They caught mullet, spot, hogfish, bluefish, drum, Spanish mackerel, and trout. Commercial fishing was the only livelihood for many. In the fall they'd go mullet fishing. They would pack the fish in salt in wooden barrels for shipping to markets in New Bern, Greenville, and Washington. My father took great care in cleaning and packing the fish to make them more desirable. They were not scaled because they would fall apart after the insides were removed. The scales helped hold the fish together. Roe would be removed and dried. It was a real delicacy, probably as good as any caviar. It was removed immediately from the fish and placed in brine for several hours.

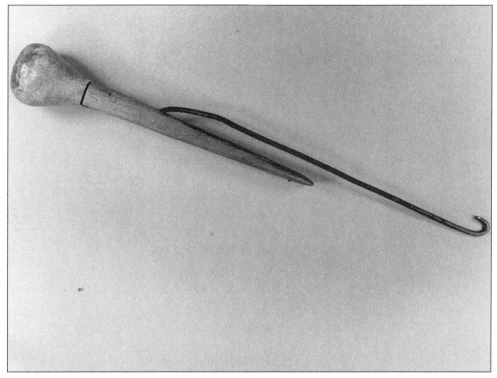

The trout sounder removed the trout's sound without having to cut open the fish. Mr. Bell invented the tool in the late 1800s and it was still in use in the early 1900s. Nettie's mother cooked the sound as well as the gizzard and liver, which were called "plucks." (Courtesy North Carolina Maritime Museum.)

Then it was spread on boards in the sun until all the moisture evaporated. When dry, they were sliced and eaten as is or fried. During World War II, Dr. Ben Royal sent dried fish roe to some of the Carteret County boys that were serving in France.

Mullet was our "chicken of the sea." The gizzard and liver was known as plucks and were good eatin'—if fried just right, they were prized eatin'. My mother ate the sound, the swim bladder of the fish that helps it maintain its buoyancy. It was different in color and shape than the roe. It was easy to get when the fish was cut open and cleaned.

In the late 1800s, fresh fish was a hot commodity and was a cash product. No one wanted to cut the fish open to get the sound. Mr. Bell of Morehead City invented a tool called the trout sounder, which removed the sound without having to cut the fish open.

It looked like a wooden blade which was inserted through a gill and pushed along the backbone to detach the sound. When the blade was withdrawn, it pulled the sound out through the gill slit with the wire hook.

A lot of things were referred to as "mullet." The train was called the "mullet line" because it was the only way fish could be efficiently hauled to market. The local newspaper was called "the mullet wrapper" because that was the way it was recycled. The first northeast wind

The Moreheads had a large house right on Arendell Street. Nettie enjoyed accompanying her father to the house to help get things ready for their arrivals and to help clean up after their departures. She loved to shoot pool in the big front room with her sisters and swing on the porch behind the lattice. Nettie spoke of the servants' quarters, which were constructed "out back" of the main house. (Courtesy John Tunnell and the Sanitary Restaurant.)

shift in the early fall was a "mullet blow." This harkened the men to their boats to go fishing. Even as late as the fifties, mullet was considered North Carolina's most valuable finfish. It was plentiful, cheap, and easy to preserve.

My sister and I often went out with Poppy. The net was piled in the stern. As the boat came around, it slid into the water. My sister would stand on the shore holding the staff. While Poppy went around with the skiff, he would hit the side with his hand making noise to scare the fish into the net.

THE MOREHEAD HOUSE

When we were old enough, we went with Poppy to the Morehead house to dust, clean, and get it ready for their holiday or summer visit. Poppy would order groceries. We would help arrange them in the storage cabinet. We'd rub the furniture with oil, which would help take away the musty smell. Their living room was much like a modern den. It was a huge room with large comfortable wicker furniture—sofas, chairs, and ottomans. It also had a pool table. My sisters and I loved shooting pool while waiting for Poppy to complete a task. But the very best things of all were the two indoor bathrooms. The toilet tanks hung on the wall. We couldn't resist pulling the chains just to be sure they worked.

If the Moreheads had not visited in awhile, Mommy would go to help. She paid attention to checking the linens—the smell and the whiteness. The Morehead servants sent sheets to the laundry. Several times the laundry didn't completely dry the linens before returning them. When Mommy opened the cabinet, the sheets were covered in black spots of mildew. The sheets went home with us and underwent Mommy's treatment with Clorox. Then they were hung on the line in sunshine. The sheets never looked whiter.

Afterward, we'd sit on the porch of the Morehead's house and look down Arendell Street. Since the house was across the street from the Atlantic Hotel, it was a fascinating place to be. We often sat and watched the people come and go. We took turns swinging and spending 30 minutes or so feeling like we were on top of the world.

Once the Moreheads arrived, they were in the hands of a small army of servants who took over the care and feeding of the family along with their guests. My father then spent his time taking out fishing parties or hunting parties depending on the season. The Moreheads were fine people and always treated us kindly. From time to time, Mr. Morehead would come by our house. He'd come up to Poppy and say something like, "Skipper, we've had a pretty good business year lately and you've done a fine job. I've brought you a little something extra." It was usually $25, which was at least a week's pay.

PROMISE LAND

Kilby Guthrie was my mother's uncle. He married my grandmother's sister, Headie Ann. He had come from the Banks after serving in the Lifesaving Service and settled in Morehead City. He bought a lot in the Promise Land area and moved his house across the sound on two sail skiffs. He opened a little grocery store on the corner of Evans and Twelfth Street, which became a gathering place and an early landmark in town. He was sort of the hero of our family.

Shackleford Banks held the strength and history of my family. My mother's and father's people were seafarers. They not only fished the waters, but they challenged the sea as lifesavers. My father's people had also been successful whalers. They instilled in my father knowledge of the sea, the sand, the dunes, the vegetation, the sun, the moon, the wind, the weather, and the local customs. After settling on the mainland, it was too painful for my parents to visit out on the Banks where they had spent their young years. At the turn of the century, they had reached the Promise Land after generations of struggle and doing without.

I remember my parents talking about the Lifesaving Service and about things that washed on the beach. Mommy didn't want to go back to the Banks but she loved shipwrecks. She would have loved to go down to the sea just to see what she could take home. She remembered "wrecking." She said it was exciting, like Christmas. They found furniture and all.

In the late 1800s most people moved off the barrier islands known as the Banks. Some moved to Down East villages or Harkers Island. Many moved to the area in Morehead City known as the Promise Land. It was between Tenth and Fifteenth Streets and was bordered by the railroad and Bogue Sound. For most, it was their first time living in close proximity to others on a lot in a planned neighborhood. However, Banks people were bound by a sea culture. They stuck together in the Promise Land even though the residents of Morehead City viewed them as being "different."

When my Grandfather Guthrie passed away leaving Grandmother with four little girls to raise on the Banks, Uncle Kib went over to Bell's Island. He brought them to live in Morehead City. It was a rescue of sorts and shows the closeness that families had. He knew the harsh life on the Banks was no place for a widow and orphans.

Living on the water was a must for my father. Our house was right on the sound. The water lapped up to the edge of our property. Poppy could put in his boat, spread his nets, and have a place for the ducks and geese he raised. He set out to fish or travel to other Down East areas any time he felt like it. Late one summer he headed to Harkers Island to visit his cousin, Julian Guthrie. He said, " Julian, I want you to build me a new spritsail. I want it this long. I want you to finish it before fall so I can take it fishing."

That's when Julian built Poppy's boat, the *Alma*. It was a sailboat but it had twarter pins, which held oar locks so he could also row it. He loved that boat and kept it until the day he died. Everybody in Morehead City and Beaufort knew the *Alma*. Most people knew my father.

There were no modern conveniences. Whatever we had to do had to be done during daylight. We didn't stay up too late at night because we could not waste fuel or wood. We were always in bed by 8:30 p.m. and earlier in the winter. We owned kerosene lamps. We thought we were living well because we had more than one lamp. I remember trimming the wicks and filling them with kerosene.

We hand washed all the clothes in a wash tub with a washboard and then hung the wash on the line to dry. We had to be mindful of the weather and the direction of the wind so soot from the train would not ruin our clean clothes. We heated water for baths and washed with Octagon Soap. I washed my hair with the soap to make it shine. Then I rinsed it with vinegar water. My braids were turned

under. If I tied them with a big, wide ribbon bow, the boys whistled at me.

Ironing was agony. We had to walk a million miles back and forth from the stove to the ironing board to keep the iron hot. A week's ironing could take all day.

Since we had an outhouse, during the night, we used a chamber pot. All houses had one in each bedroom. They were used at night, when sick, and sometimes if the weather was bad. In the morning it had to be carried out of the house no matter the weather.

My father had a Chesapeake Bay retriever hunting dog named Rex. He was a smart dog and enjoyed his life at our house when he wasn't out with hunters. Mommy bought a toy for Rex and would call his name in a certain way. He would come running out of his doghouse. She'd tell us to come to watch her. We'd go out and she'd call, "Rex," and he'd come through his door bouncing all around. We'd laugh and have fun watching the demonstration.

Alma slept in a sort of crib in my parents' bedroom for years. One night after she had put on her nightgown, she used the chamber pot. Then she mimicked Mommy's tone of voice and called, "Rex, come on." Rex went over and used the pot too. He did that every night when Alma would call him. One day Mommy said, "When you go by Dr. Royal's office tell him about Rex."

We went by to tell Dr. Royal. He couldn't believe it. The next night he came by at Alma's bedtime to watch Rex. It was true! We had a lot of fun telling the story for a long time.

ELECTRICITY COMES

The Atlantic Hotel had electricity for years before it was available to the average citizen because they had their own power plant. It was a curiosity to see

As children, the Willis girls loved going to the picture show. Taking in a movie was one of the "things to do" when Nettie was a girl. Through the years there have been several movie houses in Morehead City on Arendell Street. The City Theater is shown above (at the far left) in 1959. The building was constructed about 1911 and was the Palace when Nettie was a child. The theater building burned down in 1976. The Hardware and Building Supplies Company is on the corner. (Courtesy Eubanks/Salsi private collection.)

the hotel lit when the houses in the neighborhoods all around were totally dark. We didn't get power until I was 16 or 17 years old. Poppy was reluctant to agree to pay for something he really didn't think we needed. He was skeptical about it lasting. He just considered it unnecessary.

Progress was too strong. We got electricity! It was handled by a company from Wilmington—the Tidewater Power Company. It cost a $1.00 to $1.25 per month. They stuck wire through the outside wall, ran it along the inside wall, and up to the ceiling where the bare 40-watt light bulb hung down from a single wire.

It was fun turning on and turning off the light. It was a miracle that we no longer had to mess with the kerosene lamps and a miracle we didn't have to go to bed at dark. Electricity

changed our sense of time; it made our day longer.

We'd walk outside just to see what our house looked like in the dark with the lights on. In fact it was so much brighter than the lamps that we worried it might put our eyes out. We had real lights, not just a little dim glow.

Many Saturdays we'd go to the movies at the Palace Theatre. My sisters and I would do our chores at home and help the neighbors to raise the 10¢ admission. My sister Mamie would go and help the piano player. When the lady took a break, she would take her place at the player piano. Since she was three years older than I was and five years older than our sister Sadie, Mamie was in charge. We'd leave our house and walk over, the three of us, holding hands. We always got along and we went everywhere holding hands. The trips to the movie were totally social affairs. We didn't care what was playing. We loved it. We'd get in and then talk as hard as we could talk.

Music was important to the silent movies. Without it there would have been no sound. One piece was the prettiest, "The Trail of the Lonesome Pine." I used to sing it; everybody did. Some movies would continue the next week. That would give us something to think about and talk about for the rest of the week. Pearl White showed a girl dangling from the back of a train.

When I was about 17, there was a new theatre. They hired a girl to play the organ. I think it was Mr. Duffy Wade who owned the theatre. One day while walking home from school, I saw him and said, "Mr. Duffy, you've got to get yourself a talking picture."

And a little while after that he did. After the movie, Mamie, Sadie, and I would go straight home. We could not dit-dotter outside. After stuffing ourselves with pickles and cheese tid-bits, we were generally not hungry afterward. We'd get home, kick off our shoes, and lie around listening to Bing Crosby sing.

I didn't see a "talkie" movie until 1929. I was 18 and was living in Raleigh while attending business school. I remember it—*The Jazz Singer*, starring Al Jolson. We thought we were something, sitting in the theatre. We thought Jolson was something. I remember him singing, "Mammy."

GAMES CHILDREN PLAY

Having store-bought toys was rare. For the most part, we had to make our own fun and make up our own games. We played whoop n' hide, a type of hide-and-go-seek game. We ran back and forth in Shackleford Street as we looked for a special place to hide. When we needed more room, we went up the block to play on the corner where the streets intersected.

There were no vehicles except for the iceman, who came by occasionally. His horse pulled a white wagon with "ICE" printed on the side. If we weren't at home, we'd stick a sign on the porch saying how much ice we needed. If we left "50," the ice man would chip off one huge 50-pound chunk, carry it with his tongs, and put it in the top of our ice box on the back porch.

We had a large wooden ice box that was lined with tin. It had a drip pan with a funnel that went through a hole in the porch floor. As the ice melted, it would run all the way to the ground without wetting the food or rotting the porch floor.

We also loved playing on Poppy's net spreads when there were no nets drying. We'd hang by our arms and our legs and have a good time. Poppy liked to entertain us with a little riddle while making slash marks on paper for each syllable. He'd say:

Link to my loo, link-to-my-loo
Owned a mare—10 pounds
Paid him off seven
Bet you a shilling there's thirty and two!

It was a parlor game that we played many times. It was one of those "pass the time" things that people did using pencil and paper. First, the players had to memorize the rhyme. A pencil slash mark is made on paper as each syllable is said. The object of the game is to challenge another player by saying the rhyme fast and ending up with 32 marks on the paper. It was very entertaining and required that we read, memorize, and use our math skills.

Father was aggressive. He hated sitting around. He loved the water, nature, birds, and all. He had many birds in the backyard including pelicans, mallards, and Canada geese. His fowl were tame. They were like pets because he rescued

Churches were the center of activity for the community in the 1920s and 1930s. Every Sunday the Willis family attended Franklin Memorial Methodist Church on the corner of Twelfth and Arendell Streets. The original church was constructed of wood from the timbers of a wrecked ship. The old church was torn down and the new church was finished in 1923. (Courtesy Eubanks/Salsi private collection.)

abandoned eggs and helpless babies. He built a pen and ran a fowl orphanage. My sisters and I loved naming each one that grew up in our yard. We helped feed them cracked corn and whole grain.

They'd fly around and see us walk into the yard and land back in the yard. The ducks were the cutest. They'd go down to the landing and swim around for awhile. Then they'd come on back and stand at the gate of their pen.

By far, my fondest memories are the times we went out on the Morehead boat. It slept six, had a galley, and an engine room. Off season Poppy would take us on a sort of vacation. Right before he prepared the boat for winter, he'd take us

fishing for a few days. He'd go to Harkers Island, Marshallberg, and Cedar Island. We'd spend one or two nights on the boat.

We all got along fine with family and neighbors. We all ate well. We never heard of anyone going hungry. I remember Poppy going out fishing and dropping six fish off to each neighbor, bringing a few home for supper, salting down a few, and selling any that were left over.

ENTERTAINMENT

We attended Franklin Memorial Methodist Church at the corner of Twelfth Street and Arendell Street. It was a

Nettie's father took the family in his skiff to explore Fort Macon. It was abandoned and was overgrown by the 1920s. Nettie was fascinated by the interior of the fort, which had underbrush growing in the open areas and vines that wound around the handrails of the steps. (Courtesy North Carolina Division of Archives and History.)

In the 1920s, Bogue Banks was a long strip of land bordered by the Atlantic Ocean and Bogue Sound. The only way to the "Banks" was by boat. Even though there was no electricity, a hotel and a pavilion were constructed for day trippers and hardy vacationers. Today this area is crowded with hotels, t-shirt shops, docks, and pleasure craft. (Courtesy Eubanks/Salsi private collection.)

small wooden church when I was a little girl, and then they built a new brick building. We walked there on Sunday morning and then again on Sunday night. When I got older, I went to see if any boys were there. I have fond memories of us walking down the street to church with Mommy and Poppy and their four little girls. I can see them carrying Alma because I was six years older than she and two years older than Sadie. Mamie was three years older than me.

Entertainment was hard to come by in the late teens and early twenties. There were times that Poppy would sail us across the sound to explore Fort Macon. There was no bridge connecting Bogue Banks with the mainland and our journey to the Fort was always exciting. We went in Poppy's skiff and had to time our arrival at low tide, so the visit had to be timed just right. After World War I, the government just let it go and it grew over with vine and

trees and roots. We also liked to go over to the Fort after a heavy rain. The moat would be filled with water and we pretended we were entering a great castle.

There were wild billy goats, and on one occasion, my sister was butted down. I still remember my mother screaming.

"Us" crowd would go inside the fort. Tree roots looking like large winding veins and vines had grown in a wrapping effect around the stairways. We made like we were movie stars walking down the steps of a movie set. When we went inside, it was romantic as all get out.

When I was in my late teens during the Depression, the Civilian Conservation Corps went in and cleaned up. That was the time they were plotting the intra-coastal waterway. We met Mr. George Brooks from Beaufort, who was the county surveyor. He went to Beaufort Inlet to measure the water depths.

On Armistice Day each year, all of the elementary school students marched to the Day and Fulford World War I memorial on Arendell Street at 11 a.m. to hear Luther Hamilton. The memorial was moved from the middle of the street to its present location beside the fire and police station. The photo above shows the monument in its early glory wrapped in patriotic bunting. (Courtesy Eubanks/Salsi private collection.)

I was in my early teens when a hotel and pavilion was built on Money Island on Bogue Banks near where Atlantic Beach is today. Square dances would be held during daylight hours with musicians and a caller. It cost 25¢ to dance. There was no bridge and those who attended had to go by boat. I accompanied a young couple who let me go with them. It also used to be popular to have oyster roasts. They were held only during "R" season.

A bridge was finally built across Bogue Sound from Morehead City to Bogue Banks in 1928. Shortly afterward, a plank road was laid over the sand from the bridge to Fort Macon as a convenience to help the Coast Guard transport supplies.

Our only regular recreation generally had something to do with the church. We had services on Sundays and Wednesdays. We had get-togethers, suppers, socials, and churned ice cream to sell as a fund-raiser.

Sometimes pastors would come in town and set up a tent for preaching. We all used to go to the revivals and we'd get saved every night.

School Days

I attended the Morehead Grade School, which was first known as the Free School. We were disciplined young people. We lined up every morning and marched into the school building in a controlled and orderly fashion. If a group left their classroom, they had to line up perfectly and march to their destination. Let me tell you, the teachers didn't put up with any foolishness. The simplest infraction would have the parents at the schoolhouse. I didn't know anyone who wanted to risk a parental punishment.

Every Armistice Day on November 11, all the elementary classes were marched

Today, the American Legion Memorial stands at the opposite corner of the police and fire station across from the Fulford World War I Memorial. Unfortunately, Armistice Day is no longer observed with speeches and rallies with schoolchildren. Miss Nettie is pictured here visiting the war memorial on Memorial Day, 2000. (Photo by Frances Eubanks.)

from the schoolyard to Arendell Street where the World War I Memorial had been erected almost in the middle of the street. It was elaborately decorated in flags and bunting. We had to be in place at precisely 11:00 a.m. Mr. Luther Hamilton was the orator. He was a World War I veteran who later became a superior court judge. He always started, "In Flanders where poppys grow." He never got through the poem without people crying.

Mr. Hamilton was a wonderful speaker from Atlantic. I think there have been a lot of good speakers who have come from that area. All those Atlantic people were educated to death and that is why they were so talented. Years ago the village incorporated so they could have a tax levied to get a public school. They have more college graduates per number of population than any other place in North Carolina.

The Methodist organized the Harry North School in 1903, and I graduated after the 11th grade. My senior year was challenged by math. We had a World War I veteran who was still shell-shocked. I'm saying that because he always seemed to be in a daze and was always vague about what we should know about math. It seemed the entire class was struggling and by mid-year, we all got "Ds" on our report card—even the smart students.

We got together and took our report cards to the principal. He got us a seventh grade teacher who taught us algebra. She was excellent and we all passed.

THE FLU EPIDEMIC

The flu epidemic of 1917 did not leave any families unscathed. I was only six years old, but I remember a lot about that year. Our neighbors caught the flu and our entire family had the flu. Mommy was sick while she was doctoring us. It passed from first one and then another in our family. People were dying like flies and

several doors up the street our neighbors—a husband and wife and their little child—died. That's something I'll always remember.

Mommy was so worried about Sadie and me because we went a long time without eating. She got so concerned she asked us what we would like to eat. I thought about it for a minute and remembered seeing people in Uncle Kib's store buying pig ears and commenting on how good they were. I asked for pig ears and she went and got them. That was my first and last time eating the delicacy.

Sadie wanted baked flounder. At that time of year there couldn't have been a flounder found in the state. But somehow my mother got the flounder and fixed it for Sadie. I remember watching her pick up a piece and licking it.

THE FREEZE

Right after Christmas in 1917, the weather turned cold. One thing for sure, I remember the freeze. I don't know how we survived. Everything froze. It snowed the deepest snow that has ever occurred in Morehead City. And then the temperature stayed below 32 degrees for days and days. Our house had no insulation and our bedrooms had no heat. When it was cold, it was miserable climbing into bed. We shivered under the covers until we could get warm and then we were reluctant to get out of bed again.

I remember waking up the first morning of the freeze. I was sleeping with Mamie, and Sadie was sleeping with Mommy because Daddy had taken a hunting party out. I woke up and put my feet down off the bed. It felt weird like I had stepped in ice water. I jerked my feet up and realized that my feet were in snow. There had been a loose board and snow had sifted in throughout the night. Mommy got another board and nailed it down. When we went to the front door,

Throughout the 1920s and 1930s, migratory waterfowl attracted hunters to the Down East area. Gib Willis, Nettie's "Poppy," was a guide for Mr. Morehead and his guests. He prepared the guns, ammunition, and supplies, and loaded the boat. (Courtesy North Carolina Maritime Museum.)

we found that the snow had drifted up to the door knob. I don't know how we survived. We were so cold we stayed in bed as much as possible.

Poppy had taken out Mr. Morehead and a hunting party. Mommy was worried to death about him. He was gone for days and there was no word. He was out on an island with the men with just the food and supplies that they had loaded on the boat and taken. He put ski runners on the skiff and towed it across the totally frozen sound to Core Banks Lifesaving Station to send messages out saying they were OK. Core Sound was frozen—salt water and all.

Poppy finally got home. We went out to see what looked like hundreds of frozen geese and stuff hanging on that boat. I'm

sure we had duck and goose dinners as long as the freeze lasted, which I've heard was over 20 days.

HUNTING

From the turn of the century through the thirties, the Down East vicinity east of Beaufort became a haven for hunters. Millions of waterfowl migrated to the area because of the mild weather and abundant food. Morehead City and Beaufort were the launch points for elaborate hunting expeditions. The hunters, wealthy businessmen, politicians, and celebrities arrived by train and cars to meet their guides, secure their guns and possessions on a boat, and set

Nettie remembered her father bringing home fowl from all the hunting trips for her mother to prepare. The feathers were saved for bedding. "Our house had no insulation and the winters were colder than all 'get out'; nothing was warmer than a feather bed," Nettie recalled. (Courtesy Outer Banks History Center.)

out for one of the many hunting clubs Down East, on Harkers Island, and near various acres of Core Banks. It was necessary to hire local men who were expert sailors and who knew the hunting grounds.

Poppy was the guide for Mr. Morehead's guests. It was a tradition to hunt right after Christmas. They'd go and recreate, hunt and eat and drink, and get away from their wives and children. The wives played cards, quilted, and talked. They didn't have to have meals at a certain time and didn't have to do for their husbands. The children were on their school holiday break. It gave everyone a little break from the grind.

Nothing was ever wasted at our house. When we had too many extra fish, Poppy would salt them down. When he cleaned fowl for the hunters or for us, he saved the feathers and the down. Mommy would sew up ticking and would make bedding. When we didn't need any, she would give it away to other people. Mommy always took food to anyone she thought might be hungry or need a little help.

REMEDIES

When I was really little, people doctored themselves with mustard poultice and such. It was dry mustard mixed with flour and water. The ratio is 6:1—6 flour with 1 mustard and enough water to make a paste. Boy, it was hotter than fire. You could feel it

The south side of the 800 Block of Arendell Street, shown here in 1925, was a busy area in the 1920s. The one-story building in the middle of the photo was Fred Royal's Barbershop, where Nettie got her first hair bob. Fred was Doctor Royal's brother and served as a volunteer fireman. The Morehead City Bank was next door. The first Western Union office and the first telephone company were located in the bank building. In the foreground is the drugstore where Nettie and her friends gathered to talk and socialize. Mr. McLohon had a lunch counter in the pharmacy. Nettie remembered, "When he got a sandwich toaster we thought we had arrived." To the far left is Morton's and Marine Hardware. (Courtesy Eubanks/Salsi private collection.)

and smell it; it was sometimes overwhelming. Mommy would move it to different parts of the body as she doctored on us. It just depended on the ailment. People call me to this day asking for the recipe.

Sassafras tea was used as a kind of spring tonic. I think people in the early 1900s had allergies like they do now but didn't know what they had. The hot "tea" was not exactly good tasting, but it was soothing to a stopped-up head and a cough. There were a lot of old people who fixed the tea whether they needed it or not.

A flour mixture is a sure cure for boils. Mix flour and water in the same proportions as biscuit dough, put it on the boil, and bind it up. The water will evaporate from the flour—drying and drying.

Dr. Ben Royal was a local boy who went away to college and medical school and returned home to doctor on everyone in the county. He was a descendent of Banks people and his father had been a lighthouse keeper. He helped everybody and was also a character. He was revered until the day he died. He founded the hospital in town and worked relentlessly to treat the sick.

He was a cousin of my mother's and got along with her very well. It was hard for him to get away to make social calls yet he'd come by from time to time and sit down and visit. Those were the days no one locked their doors. If he came by and we weren't at home, he'd come on in and turn kitchen chairs upside down as a signal to let us know he had been there.

Dr. Royal and his wife did a lot for the entire community. She played the piano beautifully, especially Shubert's Serenade and gave individual piano lessons.

Dr. Royal would check out a little boy and say, "He's just the right size for fish bait." He'd wear his red huntin' cap and tell patients he was going hunting.

CHRISTMAS

Christmas was an exciting time. We couldn't wait to get out of school to get ready for the holidays. We rushed home after school and headed straight to Uncle Kib's store to get things. We made as many sweet potato pies as we could. We generally started with 15 to 20 crusts. Friends would come by and swap something they had made for one of our pies.

Sometimes we had pies until February. The weather was never perfect. It was too cold or too warm and it was hard to keep the pies fresh. Cold was better because when it was warm, the last few we ate had to have the green mold raked off the top. No one would do that today.

Poppy would hang planks from loops of rope on the back porch. It formed a multiple hanging shelf unit that we loaded with the just-cooked pies. We draped mosquito netting over to keep away any unwanted insects and pests. We left them on the porch for storage. It was the coolest place we knew and it kept them out of the way until we were ready to give them away or serve them at a meal.

On Christmas Day, we would parboil a goose or a duck. It just depended on what had been killed. I never have cared for goose so I always hoped for a duck dinner. At that time, the closest turkey was in Massachusetts. We also had corn bread, coconut cake, and sweet potato pie.

Although I do remember one Christmas when Mr. Morehead had Mr. Freeman fix us our Christmas dinner and send it over. There was a turkey, and my mother absolutely panicked. She'd never seen one and was "fit to be tied" over how to prepare it. In the meantime, I noticed that cranberries had accompanied the turkey. I had heard about cranberries and was eager to taste them. I sneaked a little taste and it was so sour I thought my mouth had turned wrong-side out. I ran to my mother and told her that having a turkey dinner was a bad idea. The whole thing must be spoiled and we needed to send it back to Mr. Freeman.

A Christmas tree was always part of our tradition. I remember when Poppy took his skiff over to where Atlantic Beach is today to a place near Hoop Pole Creek and cut down our Christmas tree. We hung tinsel, homemade decorations, red-and-green paper chains. We put real candles on the tree for decoration but we didn't light them.

In 1918 World War I ended. That Christmas, Poppy went down to the Morehead City dock where Mr. Morehead's boat, the *Reliance*, was moored. He brought home the display flags off the boat. He hung all those flags across Evans Street from one side to the other from the trees. There was over a hundred feet of flags. They were beautiful hanging there for the whole Christmas season.

We were told a lot about Santa. And did we ever get excited? We always went to a

The Atlantic Hotel, located a convenient distance from the train depot, was called the "Summer Capitol by the Sea." (Courtesy Carteret County Historical Society.)

special Christmas Eve service at the Franklin Memorial Church. When I was a little girl, I remember trying so hard to sit through the carols and the stories. But all the time I would sit there and think about Santa. We left the church one time and we were almost home and Poppy looked up and said, "There he goes. There he goes!" He let his voice build up a little and said, "Looks to me like Santa means to come right here to Shackleford Street first." He had excitement in his voice and I got so excited I ran right into the house and went to bed.

We were fortunate and always got a few gifts. It was generally nothing big, but we liked what Santa brought to us. We got a new pair of gloves, a hat, a small toy or two, and sometimes something like a kite. We looked forward to getting chewing gum and candy.

As long as Poppy worked for the Moreheads, we received gifts from them. Poppy was pleased to receive a check for $25. One year we received a fur hat and a little muff. I remember feeling rich. Once

the Moreheads gave us each a fancy doll. I mean the doll was dressed with everything including a pair of gloves; it was dressed to "the nines." My sisters and I came out with the dolls. We were so thrilled we wanted to show them to everyone.

The little girls we played with took one look at our dolls and said, "Let's not play dolls today." Of course, we were crushed. I distinctly remember the feeling of being unliked by the little girls that I thought liked me. We told Mommy and she knew what was happening. She solved our problem by saying that those were special dolls for us to play with at home. And that's what we did. We played with them when we were at home. It didn't cause any more problems. Mommy was always so wise.

FIRST JOB

In 1925 I was 14 and my father came home one day and asked if I would like to work at the Atlantic Hotel. The head

63

This 1926 image shows a peaceful scene of the 800 block on Evans Street. The city hall is shown at far left next to the fire station. (Courtesy Eubanks/Salsi private collection.)

housekeeper knew my father. She lived in a houseboat on the waterfront and asked him if he knew an energetic young person who could run up and down the steps. I worked there that one summer.

I was in "high cotton." I worked for one dollar a day and lunch, which was a big deal. The housekeepers would come up and say, "Two changes, please." Then I would count out four sheets and four pillowcases and two clean bedspreads. I'd put the dirty ones in the hamper after counting. All the linens were counted and accounted for—everyday. The laundry was sent to Braddy's in New Bern. They brought it in clean and folded and we checked it off.

Working there was an adventure. The guests were very wealthy and had beautiful clothing for every possible event. I liked watching to see what "so and so" would wear next. That was the first time I smelled perfume. I'd catch a whiff of fragrance. The ladies walked by making the air smell sweet.

I remember fires breaking out when guests set something in their room on fire from cigars and cigarettes. When a fire was reported, someone would rush down the hall and douse it with water.

The following summer I worked at the uptown tearoom called the Daisy Tea Room. Someone from Wilmington owned it. I was one of two waitresses and it was my first encounter with the public. I made $3.00 and tips per week. That money made me think I was in the big time.

I always loved to be fashionable. Working in the tearoom gave me money for a pair of stockings, money to buy something for my sisters, and then I gave my mother $2.

I wore stockings for modesty. Some women from out-of-town wore full-fashioned silk stockings by Burlington. It was so hot with no air conditioning. But how we loved those black seams. During World War II, we couldn't get hose, so my sister and I got the idea to use soft black pencil to draw a line up the back of each other's leg so it would look like a seam. Then we went on our way. The more expensive hosiery had black dots on either side of the seam at the heels. When we were using the pencil, we also added the appropriate number of dots.

A KIND OF HANGOUT

On October 30, 1927, I walked by the corner of Ninth Street about five blocks from my house. There was a drugstore there that was a kind of hangout place. It was the thing to do to walk down and get a Pepsi or a Co-cola if we had a nickel. It was right before dark and Francis Wade, Mr. Duffy's son, had three people with him. He asked us over to help entertain the people while their boat was being fixed. It was King Vidor and Lawrence Stallings, the World War I correspondent, and someone else.

We drank Co-cola and then walked down to the hospital and checked on the boat repairs. The boat was named *Tar Baby*. Stallings was married to the daughter of Mr. Poteet of Wake Forest University. They were on the way to Southport to meet Stallings's wife and father-in-law, who owned the boat.

King Vidor gave me snapshots he had made coming through the waterway. They were labeled, "photo by King Vidor featuring Lawrence Stallings." He told me that he was a big moviemaker in Hollywood. Stallings spoke up and said, "Not this week, he's not."

We walked on down to the waterfront and then Vidor and Stallings walked us home and Vidor sang, "Carolina Moon." He had the best voice.

BUSINESS COLLEGE

I graduated from high school after 11 grades. That's all there was back then. I had decided I would go to Raleigh and attend King's Business College. It was a big deal because I had wanted to take business courses and there were none offered in high school. The fee for college was $120, and Poppy was happy that I won a scholarship. Poppy paid $20 a month for my room and board.

Poppy had told the Morehead's chauffeur, Mr. Fred Bell, that I was to go on the fifth of September, 1928. Mr. Bell told him that he was to take Mrs. Morehead's sister and two children to Raleigh and that I could ride with them. I was thrilled and there I was sitting high up in the front seat of that grand car—a Packard Town car. I was up front with the chauffeur and could see the road and all the countryside. There was a special horn and the passengers in the back could speak through it and talk with Mr. Bell.

Mrs. Morehead and her children stopped at the Sir Walter Hotel for lunch. Mr. Bell took me to Mr. and Mrs. Tom Styron's house, where I stayed the year of college and then he picked up the family and drove them to Greensboro.

Raleigh was the biggest city that I had ever seen in my life. I had never been west of New Bern before then. I studied hard so I could learn everything. I had a 60 word per minute on a manual typewriter and a 90 word per minute in shorthand. My shorthand teacher was good. She had us take the Gettysburg Address. In places it sounded as though she had slowed down. I scored very high because I caught all the hyphens.

When I finished my business training, I came home and went right to work for Sheriff James Davis. He was a Republican and so was my father. The office had mostly gone to Democrats because the country was full of "died in the wool" Democrats. My father was in the minority so that explains how I got a job in the courthouse.

Working at the courthouse was exciting for an 18-year-old career woman. Nettie wrote receipts, made deposits, and served papers on those delinquent paying their taxes. Lawmen from all over the county frequently gathered there. Here is a photo of Sheriff Chadwick and Billie Williams. (Courtesy Nettie Murrill private collection.)

Being fashionable was important to Nettie and her sisters. She enjoyed designing new things to wear. She was ahead of the times when she wore these beach pajamas—it looked like a long dress but was very full pajama pants. This 1930 photo was snapped in front of the Willis's house on Shackleford Street. (Courtesy Nettie Murrill private collection.)

TAX TIME

I worked with tax preparation and payment because the sheriff was also the tax collector. I was also deputized and had to serve papers on people. I had a deputy badge that I carried in my pocket. When I'd get to the person's house, I'd say, "I can't help it, but I have this summons here, let me read it to you." Back then people didn't get mad at you like they do today.

One day Sheriff Davis asked me if I could take his car and deliver some papers. I said, "Sure," even though I had never driven. I got into the Sheriff's Chrysler knowing that all I had to do was steer and stay on the right side of the road. There were not many cars, so it was easy to stay out of the way. No one needed a driver's license. It wasn't long after that citizens could voluntarily purchase a license for 35¢.

The tax process was very interesting. I worked there as the county was becoming modern and offering services to the citizens. They were having to figure out how to levy amounts and on what to levy amounts. Back then some of the taxes went like this:

Female dogs—$2.00

Male dogs—$1.00

Cats—no tax

A boy at age 21 was considered a man and had to pay a $2 poll tax. Everything in a person's house except the stove was taxed. Considering my salary was $15 a week, taxes were high for that time. In fact, not everybody could or would pay their taxes. Very few paid them in full; however, many people would come into the courthouse and make a $3 or $4 payment toward their tax bill. The dog tax caused many people to let their pets out in the woods. They didn't want to keep them close enough to claim.

People had a hard time parting with their money because they never saw just what became of it. They just got a little piece of paper saying, "paid."

I started the summer of 1929 doing tax listings in a book as big as my living room couch. I listed name, address, receipt number, property value, tax rate, and payment in the book—all by hand. We also had a huge adding machine that we thought was so modern it must be one of the wonders of the world. It did multiplication and added long columns of figures. After all of that I wrote out a paid receipt from a special receipt book which made triplicate copies.

But all in all, a little bit of money would buy a lot of stuff. We could go to the store and buy 2¢ worth of something. Now everybody makes a million dollars a week and it doesn't do much.

During the Great Depression we paid:

5¢ per pound for coffee

6¢ per pound for sugar

15¢ per pack for cigarettes and sometimes 10¢

5¢ for a Coke or Pepsi (The Pepsi's were bigger than the Cokes.)

There was a store owner that would sometime open a pack of cigarettes and sell one for a penny. They made more in the long run by doing this but it was a

This photo, taken in 1934 at Atlantic Beach, shows Nettie wearing "The Dress." She designed and sewed it. She described it as "one of the best things I've ever made. Everyone wanted to know where I got it. I think everyone in town must have borrowed it." (Courtesy Nettie Murrill private collection.)

service for people who couldn't afford 15¢ all at once.

For Morehead City the Depression was present in the early twenties. Everything was done by hand and salaries were practically nil. There was not a great demand for things and everybody did their own thing; they fed themselves, made their own clothing, and purchased as little as possible.

If you had anything fashionable to wear, you had to make it yourself or have it made. I learned to sew by the age of nine and I was lucky that sewing became a true joy all my life. I like to design and make things for myself and my sisters. When I

This is a photograph of one of the mail boats that carried passengers, products, and mail between Morehead City, Beaufort, and the Down East communities. It was the chief mode of transportation. The Portsmouth residents also relied on the boat for the delivery of groceries, packages, and a certain amount of news from the outside world. (Courtesy North Carolina Division of Archives and History.)

was 14 and working at the Atlantic Hotel, I would spend part of my weekly salary buying 6 yards of fabric from the R.T. Willis Store on Arendell. I made a lot of things that summer and returned to school with a new wardrobe.

I remember 1929 very well. The news reported "The Crash." Everybody in town talked about "The Crash," but we truly didn't know what "A Crash" was. The stock market certainly didn't affect any of the residents of Morehead City. I'm sure it touched some of the cottagers and potential tourists, but none of the regular folks had enough money to live on—they certainly were not stock market people.

On the fateful Monday, I had added up the county's bank deposit for the sheriff,

who was also the tax collector. The auditor and I walked to the bank in Beaufort to transact business. It was either the day of or the day after "The Crash." I went to the teller and the girl says, "I'm sorry, we cannot transact further business. The President of the United States has ordered all banks closed." Then she pulled a shade down. That was it!

THE MAIL BOAT

Traveling by mail boat was a mode of public transportation as well as a method to carry and deliver goods. It was also the way to deliver the United States mail to the outlying Down East communities that were only accessible by boat. As a teenager, I would occasionally spend the weekend with my cousin who lived on Harkers Island. Her husband, Tilden Davis, captained the mail boat. I met him at the dock, paid my quarter, and set out to visit my cousin. In 1929 I went over to spend Thanksgiving with her.

After lunch on Saturday I left to return to Morehead City. We got out on the sound and it started snowing. It was really beautiful coming down all around and floating into the water. But as we continued, it started snowing harder and harder and we couldn't see our hands before our faces. Huge snow flakes were coming down in a blizzard. We could not see where we were going nor where we had been. Tilden was an excellent captain and had made the trip hundreds of times. Even he was uneasy without any landmarks to steer by. I was scared to death and thought, "I'll never see my mother again."

EVENINGS AT HOME

The Depression cramped our style. No one had any money and in Morehead City we dare not be frivolous with what we had. However, I was still living at home. Poppy and I managed to have a little weekly income and Mommy did all she could sewing for others.

I managed to get enough money and I bought a 1930 Emerson radio. We invited all of the neighbors in to listen. We spent many evenings during those hard times listening to Fibber McGee and Molly and Amos and Andy. We looked forward to the programs and sat listening and laughing.

BUMMING

Everybody nearly walked themselves to death. I was working in Beaufort but still living at home on Shackleford Street with my parents. I'd leave early and start

Nettie and a friend posed for this 1930s photograph on one of the era's prized possessions: a new car. (Courtesy Nettie Murrill private collection.)

walking across the bridge. Sometimes I could bum a ride to the county courthouse in Beaufort. Back then everybody was kind and there was no danger catching a ride with strangers. There were not many people with a car, but if one passed me walking they'd stop and would pick me up. Even the bootleggers would pick me up.

I met my husband, William, when he picked me up while I was walking to work. He was driving a school bus taking students from Morehead City to school in Beaufort. The school had burned in the fall right after I graduated. The students were assigned to the Beaufort School called the Courthouse Annex. So, there I was, walking to my job. The school bus stops and the driver says, "Would you like a ride?"

Nettie stood on the front porch of the Morehead cottage and watched the Atlantic Hotel burn to the ground. This photo was taken from the top of the hotel toward the Morehead house across the railroad tracks. The Morehead City water tower is visible in the distance. Nettie remembered the water pouring over the top as the fire department tried to put out the fire. (Courtesy John Tunnell and the Sanitary Restaurant.)

I was 18 and he was 18. He was definitely the best-looking man I had ever seen. I rode to work on the bus. A short time later I ran into him and he said, "Oh, there you are again."

That's when we started courting. Since no one had any money, we hung out at the corner drugstore. He'd walk me home the four blocks. The moon was shining every night—rain or shine.

That summer he had a job loading watermelons on freight cars at a place where Brandywine Bay is today. The famous Bogue Sound watermelons were shipped all over the United States.

So, that was that. We dated off and on for four years before we got married. He even returned to his home in New Hanover County for a while and we courted through the mail.

After we were married, William made only $12 a week. Thinking about this throws me off, especially when I go out to lunch. One day Lynn and I were having lunch and talking about the Depression. It made me think. There we were at the Sanitary spending $12 on lunch for the two of us—the same amount my husband brought home for a week of work. And those poor devils worked. I mean they had hard work from seven to five and then they had to walk all the way home for dinner.

THE FIRE

The Atlantic Hotel was an imposing structure in the heart of town. For many years the hotel provided the excitement for Morehead City and also the tourist money that was needed to provide jobs. There is not a soul who lived in Morehead City from the turn of the century until 1933 that wouldn't remember it. The fire at the hotel is one

Firetrucks were called in from the Morehead City Fire Department on Evans Street to put out the Atlantic Hotel fire. The station, shown above in the 1950s, was built in 1928 adjoining the municipal building. The building is still a landmark and currently serves both as the fire station and police station. (Courtesy Eubanks/Salsi private collection.)

of the most dramatic events that ever occurred.

I was looking right at the hotel as it was burning in 1933 the Saturday before Easter. The 12 o'clock whistle blew at the fire department and then it didn't stop as usual. It kept on blowing like all hell was breaking loose. All in our neighborhood came out of their houses and many ran toward the station to see what was happening. Black smoke was coming and blowing like waves of clouds. It looked like the whole end of Morehead City was on fire. I ran down the street. When I got to Arendell Street, I could see that it was the hotel.

All fire stations were called in—Atlantic, New Bern, and Beaufort. I went straight over and stood on the front porch of the Morehead House. When I looked out, there was Roy Eubanks standing on the railroad tracks taking pictures. The water tower was down the street from the Morehead house. The water man was pumping so hard water was running all down the tank. It looked like a big rainstorm.

The hotel burned flat in just one hour. Only the chimneys were left. It had been built of lightwood. When burning, it put out a kind of turpentine smoke. The smell was extremely pungent. The year before they had celebrated the 50th year. Everybody talked about the fire for months and wondered where the tourist would go. The year 1933 was not a good time for us to lose the tourists dollars.

The Last Morehead in Morehead City

The Moreheads stopped coming to Morehead City in 1933. My father had worked for them between 1907 and 1933.

Nettie's father bought many supplies from the R.T. Willis Store on Arendell Street. It was a general merchandise store and customers could buy overalls, boots, line, hardware, wash tubs, shoes, and canning jars. (Courtesy Eubanks/Salsi private collection.)

It was a sad day, but Mr. John Lindsay had asthma so bad that he had to stop coming. I understand that he started going to the mountains for relief. His father and mother had passed away and there was no one interested in coming to the coast regularly. There was no one to enjoy that wonderful old house.

The Moreheads offered to sell my father the house for only $4,000. That was a lot of money in 1933 but was not a great deal for that house. My father declined the offer but we all begged him to take it. We thought he and Mommy could take in boarders and do well. Schoolteachers and visitors were always looking for places to stay.

Poppy said, "No." He didn't want to have the upkeep. He knew what was involved after having been the primary caretaker all those years. So, the house was sold to Doctor Thompson.

A little while after that, Mr. John and his sister Catherine wanted to give Poppy the yacht. He was such a practical man that he was opposed to the gift. They wrote up papers and sent it to him. Their letter said, "Because you have been faithful . . ."

Poppy said, "I've had enough of that upkeep." He sold the yacht for $1,000 and used part of the money to have a nice little fishing boat built in Marshallberg and equipped it with a snapper engine. His upbringing had just been too practical for him to own anything elaborate, but he had a good time with the snapper.

Being a boatman was Poppy's thing but going offshore in a yacht all day wasn't his cup of tea. He enjoyed taking the Moreheads anywhere they wanted to go, but when he was not out with them, he enjoyed a small boat and the fishing in the sound much more. He sometimes said that going offshore meant bigger fishing adventures. He had to put up with many guests needing help with their bait and sticking him with their hooks.

CAMP

In 1933 or 1934, Poppy helped Mr. Pat Crawford from Kinston at Camp Morehead. It was first a boys-only camp and then it opened for girls. Poppy cut custom sails for the little Comet sailboats and taught sailing. He'd buy lightweight canvas from the R.T. Willis Store on Arendell Street. He took it home and laid it out on the ground and cut the three-cornered sail pieces by eye-balling them. He never had a pattern. He'd tell us what piece went where and Mommy and I would cut and sew it. The first year of camp required a great deal of work because we had more than 12 sails to make.

In the mid-forties, Poppy raced the *Alma* and won year after year. Out of four or five years he was only beaten one time—by Dr. Robinson from Burlington. Then he beat Dr. Robinson and did not lose again. After that Poppy was somewhat of a sailing legend.

A few years ago the yacht club invited my sister Alma and me to their 50th anniversary and they honored our father. He would have liked it; not the honor as much as the fact that he was still known as an outstanding sailor.

HURRICANE SEASON

Hurricanes have always been part of our history. As a child, they were merely an inconvenience. When we were under a hurricane alert, it was boring, to say the least. It was hot inside a boarded-up house. We depended on our kerosene lamps, our chamber pots, and in my youngest years, salted fish.

The Hurricane of 1933 is one that people still refer to. It washed over the Banks and opened a new inlet where Diamond City was located.

Poppy stopped by the bank to read over the weather report telegram that the dot-dash man, Jimmy Rabon, had received via telegraph. The weather telegram was at the bank every day for residents to read. Western Union had an office there.

The main message that day was to Gordon Willis, the display man, who manned a tall tower, like a radio tower, where he raised storm flags. He was instructed to hoist a northeast storm warning for Cape Lookout and north.

My father walked on home and walked down the narrow path beside our house to the backyard. I was sitting on the back steps writing to William, who was then my sweetheart. Poppy said we should prepare to board up our windows on the east side of the house because there was a storm headed our way and it looked like it was going to be serious.

I went on writing, "It looks like we have a bad time coming. But it's a nor'easter which will be bad enough but shouldn't hit us too hard."

It turned out to be a hurricane which gave us a direct hit. We had a lot of wind and rain but the poor people Down East suffered something terrible. The Pamlico flooded on the north side. Boats, buildings, and livestock were washed away and several people lost their lives.

In October 1954 it was Hurricane Hazel that hit Morehead City hard. When it washed through the inlet, the Bogue Sound looked more like the Atlantic Ocean. That was because the wind came in from the southeast. The tide came all the way up to our back door and stood in the alley. I remember watching it and thinking our house might just wash away. Hurricanes were particularly an inconvenience. We didn't miss electricity but we had to fill every receptacle with water, use our chamber pots, and when our ice ran out we ate a lot of bread and salt fish. As the storm raged, we entertained ourselves in a hot, stuffy, dark, boarded-up house

The losses back in those days were nothing like today. We never erected docks or left boats or anything in the water or on the sand. Nowadays people construct walkways to the water. It's silly to do that to begin with if you're at the coast. People simply can't challenge the weather.

WORLD WAR II

World War II caused a lot of changes in town and put Morehead City in the modern age. U-boat activities off our shore put the War on our doorsteps and caused us to be conscious and concerned about the War everyday. It was ever on our minds that Germans might actually come ashore and capture Morehead City and Beaufort. From where we lived, we could see the beach horizon. We actually saw flames and smoke from the torpedoed ships that were on fire. We took many precautions. Shelters were established all around town. The air raid siren would go off and we were always relieved to find out it was a drill—yet we were never sure. We had to hang black curtains in our windows so that light would not show from the houses at night and cause the shoreline to be outlined.

There were no streetlights and the car headlights were shaded with heavy black paper so that the beams would be directed down to the pavement. The coast was blacked out as much as possible. There were air raid wardens all over town with flashlights and wearing a white helmet. Posters were put in public places saying something like, "Do not discuss the conditions. These walls have ears." We were all good cautious citizens.

The opening of Cherry Point Marine Base in Havelock and the location of a seaplane base at the old National Guard Camp at Camp Glenn caused more people to arrive in the county than there was available housing. Everyone who could took in boarders. In some cases, people moved in with relatives freeing up a few

houses as rentals. My husband and I bought a house for $25 that we moved to a lot. It didn't take long for many of the vacant lots in Morehead City to be filled with houses. Many of the quickly constructed World War II houses are still standing alongside original Promise Land houses.

There was a seaplane base located down the sound from our house. We could hear the amphibious planes taking off and landing from missions searching for U-boats. I remember them going over while I was hanging laundry and it got me thinking that I needed to be careful how I hung the clothing. I didn't dare risk mixing up the clothes. I hung all the colored clothes together and the white clothes together just to be sure the pilots wouldn't think I was sending a signal.

My aunt lived down the street and in the summer she fought mosquitoes with a vengeance. She built a fire in a smoke pot and then put a damp fabric over the flame and lifted it up creating clouds of smoke that kept the insects away. It was an old-fashioned remedy even back then; but it worked. Once a military man came and asked her what kind of signals she was sending. We teased her the longest. I don't think she ever smoked up her yard after that—mosquitoes or not.

In 1942 we had to go to the schoolhouse and sign up for ration tickets. I think I still have a few. It paid to be conservative—not to be a spendthrift. We had neighbors who didn't use sugar. I swapped my shoe rations for their sugar.

Dr. Royal first had a hospital on the second floor of a building on Arendell Street and then he built a real hospital on the Bogue Sound waterfront. He chose the location because everyone traveled by boat. There was a hospital dock. When the sick arrived by boat, they could easily be rushed into the hospital. During the War many wounded and dying men were

Good friends celebrated Nettie's 89th birthday at the Sanitary Restaurant. From left to right are the following: (seated) Burke Salsi, Miss Nettie, Lydia Haley, and Nannie Haley; (standing) Frances Eubanks, Connie Mason, Bo Salsi, Lynn Salsi, and Brian Salsi. (Courtesy Frances Eubanks.)

picked up in the ocean and brought to Dr. Royal. No one worked harder for the war effort. Dr. Royal was known to help carry wounded men into the hospital.

THE CHANGES

After the war more people came to Morehead City and to Carteret County. The beach that started out being a big sand bar became an important destination for people. It used to be just in the summertime. Now they come from all over almost all of the year. In the summer I just try to stay home and stay out of the traffic.

Outsiders have always come to Eastern North Carolina and commented on the way we speak. I thought of a few special words and expressions that I think might be unique:

Airish: chilly

Blue million: a lot

Cattywampus: crooked not square

Co-cola: how most people referred to Coca-Cola

Crowd: a group doing the same activity or a group of people who are known to stick together, i.e. "That crowd over at the beach."

Dingbatter: outsiders, especially tourists

Directly or t'rectly: soon

Dit-dotter: waste time, i.e. "We couldn't dit-dotter around."

Fetch up: get

Flood tide: unusually high tide

Goaty: stinks, get away from me; you're smelling goaty

Guano: fertilizer from fowl such as chicken

Gutful: stomach full from overly eatin

Hard blow: strong wind

Hear tell: heard

This photo was taken on March 26, 2000, at the reception at the Carteret County Historical Society for the Images of America title Carteret County. *(Photo by Frances Eubanks.)*

Heist: to lift

Kin: relatives

Liable to: likely

Mash: refers to pushing a button

Meddlin': not minding your own business

Mommicked: aggravated in the worst way

Nor'easter: wind blowing from the northeast

Over to the beach: the way we referred to activity on the Atlantic Ocean beaches

On account of: because

Reckon: suppose

Right as rain: expression for right, as in correct

Skeeter hawk: dragonfly

Yonder: there or over there

EDITOR'S NOTE

To know Nettie Murrill was to be blessed. I spent seven years and hundreds of hours talking to her about everything—the wind, hurricanes, the cost of a new car, the value of a dollar, how to raise children, politics, religion, and how to rake the leaves in the front yard. Nothing escaped Miss Nettie; she was one of the smartest women I've ever known.

By far our mutually favorite topic was Morehead City. We strolled the waterfront, sat on benches, had lunch with friends, dropped in at the Carteret County Historical Museum, hung out on the patio of the Atlantic Beach Sheraton, drove by her childhood home on Shackleford Street, visited Harkers Island (only in good weather), ate French fries at Kentucky Fried Chicken, and shared opinions of everything over ice cream cones at the Dairy Queen. We both loved to talk, but not at the same time. I quickly found out that anyone with the last name "Willis" or who was descended from anyone with that name were relatives.

If a month went by Miss Nettie would call and say, "Where are you? It's time for a little 'F–U–N.'" Often I dropped everything, drove five hours, and showed up on her doorstep the next day. She always said, "Are you crazy?"

I love wit, wisdom, and authenticity. Miss Nettie was all of that and more. She loved people and they loved her. She often told me that she knew I had heard her tell the same story a "blue million" times and I was the only person who had never said, "I've already heard you tell that."

Nettie told me to write fast and come back soon. I'd say, "What are you talking about?" She'd say, "Lynn, I'm 85!" When she reached 89, I knew Nettie surely must have a clear ticket to 100. She didn't.

I loved "driving Miss Nettie" and so did Burke, Bo, Brian, and our dog, Maxine.

We finished crafting her story one week before she passed away. When I put my pen down, Nettie looked at me and said, "Learning the hard way is for the birds."

—Lynn Salsi

CHAPTER THREE

PORTSMOUTH

CLARA SALTER GASKINS AND MARIAN BABB

A GOOD PLACE TO LIVE

My father, Theodore Salter, was born on Portsmouth Island in 1880. His parents had moved there from Sheep Island, which was about a half mile up the banks on the other side of Warren Gilgo's Creek. He was orphaned at the age of seven and was raised by one of his eight brothers and sisters. Mama said the older brothers and sisters raised him, but they were busy with their own families and trying to make a living. If they tried to make him do something he didn't want to, he didn't do it. That's why Papa didn't get much schooling; he went fishing instead. But he was a good man. He believed in the Golden Rule.

My mother, Annie Dixon, was also born on Portsmouth. Her older brother, Joe Dixon, was married to Papa's older sister, Lorena Salter. I'm sure they had known each other all their lives. Papa had to go off the island for a marriage license. They got married in the Methodist-Episcopal Church South on August 17, 1904. Papa was 21 and mother was 18. They spent their entire lives in Portsmouth, except for a very short period of time when they moved to Fisher Street in Morehead City and then returned to Portsmouth.

My father owned the general store in Portsmouth. It was a white frame structure with a wide front porch. It was the gathering place in the community. Men would come and sit on the porch, whittle, and talk. They'd talk about the weather, their boats, and the best place to fish.

My mother, Annie Dixon Salter, was the postmistress. The post office was located on the left side as patrons entered Papa's general store. She had many open places that served as a type of mail-slot where she sorted the letters. The mail arrived by mail boat every weekday afternoon. Henry Pigott would go out and meet the mail boat. He would then bring it in a mail bag from the dock to the post office in a wheelbarrow. Boxes and parcels would be

Clara's father, Theodore Salter, owned the general store. It is still standing at the end of the path from the haul over dock. Her mother, Annie Salter, was the postmistress. The post office was located inside the general store in the left front corner. The store was the center of the community and the gathering spot every day, as most of the residents came to wait for the arrival of the mail boat. (Photo by Frances Eubanks.)

stacked on top. She rarely had the chance to file the mail. Most residents were already waiting at the post office when Henry came up. Mama mainly called the names out and handed them their letters and packages through an opening in her post office.

The post office was an exciting place to visit. Mama put up posters that were sent in by the federal government. There was an "Uncle Sam Wants You" poster and "Most Wanted" posters. Every now and then, there was an advertisement announcing bids on mail carrying. Before Henry got the job, Carl Dixon had carried the mail for years. The person with the lowest bid got the contract. Carl told Mama that he liked the job but he was too afraid to go up on his bid. When Carl quit, Henry took over. They were both paid by the federal government on a monthly basis. One thing was for certain;

Mama took great care in keeping people out of the official post office space. None of the children or grandchildren were allowed in.

Papa was a "Jack of all trades," as were most of the men who lived on Portsmouth. He kept his store, did commercial fishing, and worked as a hunting guide. He needed to have that many jobs in order to provide for the family.

Portsmouth was always a pretty place. Many people grew flowers and all had gardens. We had lilies on each side of the steps. Tiger lilies and daffodils were planted in many yards around the fences and doorsteps. In fact, tiger lilies almost grew wild.

Daddy loved the front porch. It was nice and breezy. We spent many good times out there visiting with neighbors. Some people had swings but we didn't. I

The post office was located in an enclosure at the front of the store, where Annie Salter sorted the mail and packages. Many residents were waiting when Carl Dixon, and later Henry Pigott, brought the mail from the mail boat. She received the mail bag and then called out the names of the recipients, handing the letters through a small window. (Photo by Frances Eubanks.)

don't know why we didn't. Back then, there was no special furniture for a porch. We just dragged chairs out from inside the house and put them back inside.

Our house was large and comfortable and had two chimneys. It had been built by Uncle Joe Dixon, who sold it to my father. It had a full second story with four bedrooms. Daddy moved it to its present location from "up the beach" so that mother wouldn't have so far to walk to her work at the post office. That's when he added the kitchen and remodeled the second floor. There were a lot of windows to let in the light. There were heavy wooden shutters that would be pulled to cover them during storms and hurricanes. All of the houses were built to withstand storms. They were built well. I never remember one being damaged.

Inside, the rooms were spacious. The dining room had a round table and straight chairs. There was a pie safe where we stored homemade preserves. It was one of the warmer rooms in the house because a coal stove was in there. Since there was no heat in the upstairs, mother put a daybed in there for resting.

We had an inside kitchen with two doors. We had to be sure one of the doors was closed when we used the oil stove; we couldn't have a draft. The sink was under the window with a hand pump in it that pumped water directly from the cistern outside of the kitchen window. It was good when Papa built the big water tank to have as a second cistern in case of lack of rain. Most of the houses had a summer kitchen that was separate from the rest of the house. It was meant to keep the heat out of the main house and be a protection against fire.

Papa had a storage shed out back where he kept tools, nets, and a saddle. I'll

Most of the houses had a summer kitchen that was detached from the house and was a separate structure. This kept the heat out of the main house, and allowed it to be spared if the kitchen caught on fire. This is a back view of the Salter's two-story house. (Photo by Frances Eubanks.)

Theodore Salter had an outbuilding constructed next to his house in which he stored his equipment and supplies. The building is still standing and now houses a generator to run electricity for the needs of the Cape Lookout National Seashore. (Photo by Frances Eubanks.)

always remember how careful he was with his tools. They were hard to come by. He kept a horse. Although he built a fence, he sometimes let him run. He used the horse with a cart to haul stuff. He had a stable near his store and kept him tied on a rope so he'd be handy in case he needed to hook him up to haul. (Clara Salter Gaskins.)

When Granddaddy Henry Babb had a store, he'd send his son, Little Henry, up the banks to deliver a barrel of flour. Henry would hitch up the horse named Ol' Jim and go for a delivery. When Henry saw Grandmother putting beans on to cook, it would make him happy, because he'd know he was having beans for supper. He just loved her beans. As he made his way, he'd pass Miss Hubb's house. She'd tell everyone she could hear Henry singing "Good ol' beans for supper" at the top of his voice and she'd know what the Babbs were having for supper. (Marian Gray Babb.)

We had to hand wash all of our clothes in a wash tub on the back porch. The porch was constructed without rails and was the right height to place the tub on it so the person washing could stand on the ground and would not have to bend over too far. We dried the things on an outdoor clothesline and laid things over the fig bushes if we ran out of line. When they dried, we carefully folded everything. Most things had to fit into drawers and trunks. There were few closets in houses at that time. Our Sunday clothes were kept in the upstairs closet.

We all had feather beds. When Papa went hunting, he would save all of the feathers when cleaning the fowl. The feathers had to be completely seasoned. They had to be completely dry so there was no smell. The geese and other fowl were picked and the feathers were put in a flour barrel and then a tote bag was pulled over. They kept all the flour barrels

This is an aerial view of Portsmouth Village. The Dixon/Salter house is visible in the foreground, and Marian Babb's residence is visible near the Portsmouth Methodist Church. (Photo by Frances Eubanks.)

to store things in. Later, the feathers were put in cloth bags and tied to the rafters in the attic until we were ready to use them. We kept a lot of things in the attic that we didn't want to throw away. We kept everything we ever got in case we needed to use it. In the twenties and thirties no one wasted anything.

We'd take the feather beds and lay them on the floor by the window in summer. We liked sleeping there to catch the breeze and hear the ocean.

When I got married, Mama made me a couple of feather pillows and a few quilts.

The myrkle bushes were native to the island. The branches were used to fan the mosquitoes and other biting insects. The swishing sound of the branches being fanned could be heard in church. (Photo by Frances Eubanks.)

People talk about the big mosquitoes when they speak about Portsmouth. We had mosquitoes, no see 'ums, and green heads. At various times and conditions they would be a bother. Mostly, we would have an ocean breeze which kept them away. If they got bad, we'd fix smoke pots near the house. We'd burn old rags and that would make more smoke than flame. We also used myrkle branches to swat mosquitoes away. We'd also paint our screens with kerosene to keep no-see-ums from coming into our house. We also had insect protection from cicadas which were known mosquito eaters. People would sit on their porches with a branch and the fanning would keep the insects away. During World War II, the government did spraying. Most of the underbrush was kept out so the breeze could come

through. Back then, we could stand on our porch and see people at the Coast Guard Station. (Clara Salter Gaskins.)

THE DEPRESSION

Times were hard during the Depression and some families left the village to seek work elsewhere. They never returned even after things got better. The government enacted a work program and got the WPA to build up the roads. They dug ditches along the side of the road. They threw the sand up in the road. That's the way they built the road up. (Clara Salter Gaskins.)

The Lifesaving Station was a security to the residents of Portsmouth from its construction in 1894. During World War II, it was activated as a Coast Guard station. (Courtesy Outer Banks History Center.)

WORLD WAR II

The Lifesaving Station was an important look-out station during World War II. The Coast Guard had a number of boys there. They were in for a lot of surprises. Even at that time, we were living in the past. Because of the shallow water, they had to be put overboard and wade to shore. Many had their feet cut from the oyster shells in the water; they had to learn to wear boots or take precaution.

We looked strange to those men arriving. Most of the ladies wore aprons. They had to get used to seeing the way we dressed. We heard that some of the sailors threatened AWOL. Eventually they settled in and enjoyed the village and hearing about what used to be here.

When the bombing started off the shore, we knew about it. After dark the bombs were so close that the windows would tremble. It was not pleasant and felt as big as an earthquake. We never saw bodies wash ashore. We heard that every now and then a body would wash ashore at a camp that was built near the Pilentary Hunting Club about 10 miles down the island.

The Coast Guard had sub-stations near Morehead City, Core Banks, and Cape Lookout. Any wounded sailors were pulled from the water and taken to Morehead City to the hospital by boat. (Marian Gray Babb.)

I met my husband, Joe, when I went to Georgia to help my sister Mabel after she was married to John Midgette, who served

The beach is a mile walk from the Lifesaving Station. During World War II, island residents were not allowed to be on the beach after dark. The Coast Guard men patrolled the beach 24 hours a day. (Photo by Frances Eubanks.)

in the Coast Guard. We were married in 1939. Shortly after World War II began, Joe and I returned to Portsmouth for a visit with Papa, Mama, Mabel, and John, who was then serving at the old Coast Guard station that had been recommissioned. Joe went over to the Coast Guard Station every morning to see John and went into the lookout, the cupola type room on top of the station He was amazed. Every morning when he returned from the station, he said he saw a ship burning offshore.

He said, "I could see them right out there." In fact, ships came in so close to shore that we could see the men walking around on the deck. (Clara Salter Gaskins.)

During the war, the beach, which was about a mile from the village, was patrolled 24 hours a day. They had some men patrolling on horseback. They had a stable and a corral and loads of horses for the horse patrol. They also had patrols that walked up and down the beach. One went north and the other one went south.

Once my brother was on patrol and saw strange men on the beach. He was a scared man. He thought that they must be Germans who had come ashore from a U-boat. He approached the men and found out they were government surveyors. He stopped them and made them sink to the ground while he made a call. He plugged a phone into a post on the beach and called the Coast Guard Station. Then he

Clara Salter Gaskins and Marian Babb are shown here aboard the Green Grass *travelling from Atlantic to North Core Banks enroute to Portsmouth. After the village was no longer a viable community, they returned for long visits during the summer months. Clara's daughter Frances and son-in-law Larry Eubanks drove them and their provisions "down the banks" to Portsmouth in a four-wheel drive. (Photo by Frances Eubanks.)*

marched them to the station. That's when he found out they were American geological surveyors.

No one was allowed to walk on the beach after dark. That was a hardship for us. We were young and were used to going over to the beach and walking with our friends. One night three of us—me, Lee, and a friend—decided to go. We left a little too late and it became dusk. We had not given ourselves time to get back. We headed back but we were not worried because we had walked right past the Coast Guard Station and we knew they had seen us.

We were halted! It scared us to death! No one ever caught us again! (Marian Babb.)

EDITOR'S NOTE

Clara Bell Salter Gaskins and Marian Grey Babb shared a common bond. They were born on and grew up on Portsmouth Island, an island off the coast of North Carolina across the inlet from Ocracoke and also part of the Outer Banks. Both women were known for being independent and determined, traits which surely were passed to them through generations of family who stuck it out and coped with the elements. They possessed a strong faith, which was honed from being face-to-face with the elements with no distractions interjected by today's society.

The little one-room wooden frame church on Portsmouth puts up no facade, no pretension to be anything other than a place to connect with the Almighty and be blessed. Neither Clara nor Marian had time for facades—they had to be taken as they were: precious jewels formed from the pressures of island living and from exposure to daily lessons in survival.

During adulthood, their paths separated; Marian remained on Portsmouth to care for her aunt. Clara met and married a Georgian and raised four girls. The island subsequently was taken over by the government and became part of the Cape Lookout National Seashore Park. Marian, her Aunt Addie, and Henry Pigott were the last remaining residents. With the death of Henry in 1971, Marian and her aunt moved to Beaufort. Marian retained a lifetime right in her home on Portsmouth, and to her, it was *home*. She always looked forward to returning in the summers to stay in her house.

Over the years, Clara was a working mother. Yet she made the time to bring her daughters to Portsmouth to visit their grandparents, instilling in them a lifelong love, appreciation, and fascination for the island. There they learned how things were done without the modern conveniences they were used to on the mainland. This empowered them with self-confidence that comes from knowledge.

In later years, Marian's health declined and she became apprehensive about making her summer journeys alone. Clara returned with her. Marian lived for those trips. Clara always said she went so her daughter Frances would have the opportunity to take photographs. There was an eager anticipation of the trips. After their arrival, there was a peacefulness in Clara's demeanor that came as she walked the paths, spent long hours talking with old friends, and sat in the porch swing at Marian's. She protested that she had no desire to return to the hardships of island living—but she was home.

—Frances Gaskins Eubanks

CHAPTER FOUR
PORTSMOUTH
MARY SNEAD DIXON

THE NEW TEACHER

I went to Portsmouth as a schoolteacher in 1916. They needed a teacher, and I traveled all the way from my home in Swain County, as far west as one can go in North Carolina. It was an adventure for me, but I wanted to teach.

In 1889, I was born Mary Snead in Louisburg, Kentucky, where I lived on a farm with my family. My father was originally a farmer. Then we moved to Tennessee and then during my high school years we lived in Mississippi. Shortly after that, we moved to Cullowhee, North Carolina, and I studied there.

I met Mr. Emmet, the Carteret County superintendent of education, at a meeting of state superintendents. He was inquiring about hiring a spare teacher in Carteret County. There was only six months of school at that time, and my school in Bryson City was to be closed after the first six months. I didn't mind

having a second teaching job for six months.

I decided I would teach in Portsmouth, and Mr. Emmet was in agreement to let me finish in Bryson City first. I was excited to go because I had never been to the ocean.

Mr. Emmet wanted to know if I had ever heard of the island? I told him I had, because my father had a friend in Bryson City who'd been hunting on the coast and had told my father he knew about the place.

I got to Beaufort too late to catch the boat and I had to spend the night there. I left early the next morning on the regular mail boat and it took all day. I was the only passenger. There was no place to eat or anything. I had to take what I wanted or needed with me or simply do without.

When we got to Portsmouth, it was low tide. Mr. Alfred Dixon waded out in boots to receive the mail and supplies. He looked at me and I realized he didn't know there was a passenger. He

Mary Snead arrived in Portsmouth in 1916 and taught her first classes in the old school on Straight Road, which was located half-way between Portsmouth and Sheep Island. This is a picture of her first class. The building is no longer standing. These students include the following: Charlie Salter, Ally Ricci, Floyd Gaskins, Elmo Gilgo, Russell Dixon, Ernest Salter, Elsie Salter, Leona Babb, Madelene Harris, Ethel Gilgo, Estel Dixon, Virginia Salter, Neva Salter, Maybell Bragg, Mabel Salter, Mary Snead, Annie Mary Bragg, Alvin Harris, Tom Gilgo, Levin Fulcher, Henry Babb, Tom Gilgo, James Gilgo, and Nora Roberts. (Courtesy Frances Eubanks private collection.)

commented on not having extra boots to wade ashore.

I saw him take off the mail, the groceries, and the packages. All the time I was thinking, "How am I to get there?"

After unloading the things, he came back to the boat and turned around and picked me up. He carried me to shore and set me down.

IMPRESSIONS

My first days on Portsmouth were memorable and the things I experienced took a lot of getting used to. I was so far from home. I didn't know what to expect. Before that day I had never seen a man barefooted nor one who went to the dinner table without a coat and tie. The people talked with a kind of brogue. I found out that someone could tell the difference from one area to another area by their type of brogue.

The houses were neat and clean, and the people kept up with their appearance and style through the Montgomery Ward and Sears and Roebuck catalogues. The ladies were "perfect" housekeepers. Each one had to keep house and tend to the children.

People visited one another and sat on front porches and talked. I stayed with Miss Jane Dixon, who kept extra rooms for guests. She was the most educated illiterate person I've ever known. She got her education through her ears.

Croquet was one of the chief amusements. Sarah Roberts was the best player. I learned the game from her and we played in our yard and at Sarah's outside the fence. Since I taught, we had no regular schedule, we just played whenever we had time. Each one of us had our own set. It was a very pleasant way to pass the time away.

Uncle Theodore Salter owned a general store, and his wife, Annie, ran the post office on one side of the store. The store was the gathering place for everyone. The men sat on the porch and talked and whittled. When I first saw it, the porch was all whittled up where the men had sat and cut on it.

Even in 1916 people talked about the way things used to be. Mr. Sam Tolson was the oldest resident. He remembered when there were large trees out on the ocean where the breakers are now. The people remembered about whaling days and shipwrecks.

Once a whale washed ashore. By that time I was married and had children. They were big enough to run down to the beach to see it. The whale was big. There was a car parked on one side of the whale. I was on the other side with my Kodak camera. When I got my photographs, I noticed that I couldn't see the car. People came from other places to see the whale. I later found out that the outsiders came to get the ivory. Portsmouth didn't get the benefit. It was a pity.

There were several stores on Portsmouth where we could buy certain things. They carried mostly basic items. The mail boat brought those things we couldn't get from the store and we regularly relied on Sears and Roebuck.

I enrolled 40 children for the first class I taught on Portsmouth. That was in 1916. Prior to my arrival the children usually had only a two- or three-month school term. From that time on, the gradual decline in students there could be marked by each storm.

Yet I never closed my door on students who wanted to join the classes. Many older children couldn't afford to go off the island to attend high school, so I also taught high school subjects when necessary.

Our school was a one-room building. The teacher's desk was at the front and there was a blackboard behind. I started classes each day at 8:30 by ringing a hand bell. Then we always had a prayer. I taught all the subjects to each student, regardless of the grade.

The children had a desk with inkwells. They had copybooks for writing. I stopped them if they were using supplies in the wrong way because paper was valuable back then. The textbooks we used were the ones regularly scheduled by the county. I didn't get to choose. All of our supplies and books were taken care of in Raleigh. When I needed them, I would order and they would arrive by the mail boat. At the end of each term, I sent the school records to Raleigh.

I didn't have any attendance or discipline problems, yet I used a switch when necessary. I never had a dunce stool.

We started the morning reciting verses from the Bible. I remember one little one whose daddy was in the Coast Guard and couldn't talk plain. She liked to say, "If ya' love me keep my 'mandments." After that, we'd have English class. But with so many grades and classes to teach, I sometime didn't have much more than five minutes to spend on each subject with each grade. I tried not to expect too much from the students outside of class more than a little bit of homework. Their families worked

This is the second school building constructed on Portsmouth. It was used until the early 1940s, when there were no longer enough students in the area to conduct classes. The building recently received a fresh coat of paint by volunteer members of the Friends of Portsmouth Island. (Photo by Frances Eubanks.)

hard. And many men worked night and day. The children had to help around the house and many boys learned to fish at an early age.

We took a break at lunch. Some students brought their lunch from home which was whatever they could get, usually leftovers. Others went home for lunch and then returned. We spent all of our school days in the classroom. Field trips off the island were unthought of.

Sometimes the children taught me. There was a certain heritage and history of the island which had been established in the early 1700s. They knew about the state before North and South Carolina were divided. They could tell about the Carolina province and Governor Wallace (honorary title), who was buried in a Portsmouth cemetery. I was new, so the students knew more than I did about the community.

The last year I taught on Portsmouth was in 1943; I had two students. They were the children of Mabel Midgette and her husband, John, who was in charge of the Coast Guard Station. There were still a number of people living on the island at that time, but the older children attended school off the island and many had grown up and were not school age.

ABNER

I met Abner when I was visiting Sarah Roberts Styron. She was living at Miss Janes's then. Her mother had died and Miss Jane looked after her as though she was her own child. Abner wanted an answer about marriage after I had completed the first term, before I left Portsmouth. I wasn't sure about living way out there on an island, so I went back home to Bryson City and taught for six months. Living in Portsmouth was not easy. Yet in 1916, living in the rural mountain community of Bryson City was not easy either. After I completed my teaching in the mountains, I returned to Portsmouth.

All who lived on the island had cisterns to collect rainwater for drinking and bathing. If a big storm came, it would fill the cistern with salt water. Most people took precautions to keep this from happening. We depended on the artesian well at Casey's Point where there had been a fish factory. That well was full of sulfur, but when the sulfur evaporated, we could drink the water.

After I married, I went to Abner's home, which was not far from the first schoolhouse. Even then, all the houses from up the banks were gone. Some people had moved theirs closer to the village. I continued teaching, which was unusual for a married woman of the time. The school building was only heated by a pot-bellied stove. It was always cold. Abner never let me go out in the cold. He would go over early and have the room as warm as possible by the time I arrived to teach.

Our only transportation was on our own two feet or by boat. We walked all over the island. We never had a car; there were no roads, only wide packed paths. To drive down the banks was to go over rugged terrain. We couldn't use a car. I think that Harry Dixon, Uncle Theodore Salter, and Walker Styron were the only three with cars. I know that Mr. Styron took his car off the island from time to time and went on trips. We never even had a horse.

When my two children were born, it kept me home for awhile. I think Annie

Mae Edwards was the name of the teacher who came from Tennessee to take my place. She knew about the job at Portsmouth because she had been teaching in Ocracoke. She taught six months on Ocracoke and then came across the inlet and taught in Portsmouth for six months.

FREE RANGING LIVESTOCK

Many had livestock—free ranging. When my son was a baby, we had one cow and also some chickens. Our cow ran free. Once when water was scarce, one wild cow was found with its head as though it was trying to get a drink. It was so thirsty it drowned in a well. The water was so far down that the cow couldn't get out.

In those times I would go out to find our cow and give it water. I stood out there with a big tub and I would pour out water. The cow would drink as long as I could bail it out.

We eventually decided to get rid of our cow. Ticks became so bad and my husband didn't see putting her through the dipping vat. The State of North Carolina made every cow go through it. Abner was so attached to the cow he thought it was much more merciful to put her out of her misery.

They had regular livestock round-ups whenever the ticks were bad. They'd bring the animals in for dipping. The vat was not far from our house. The animals were immersed in a solution and that was to kill the ticks.

The village was situated on the end of an island about a mile off the Atlantic Ocean in a marshy area. There were plenty of mosquitoes there—plenty! We used smoke pots to keep them away when there was no breeze. We'd build a fire and smother it down. We also used myrkle bushes to swat mosquitoes away.

Most of the men in Carteret County engaged in commercial fishing. Salt mullet was a desirable cash product for those who lived on Portsmouth. Many men had small spritsail boats for fishing, hauling, and taking their families out for a sail or over to Ocracoke or Cedar Island. This photo was made on the sound side way down the banks close to the Cape Lookout Lighthouse. (Courtesy North Carolina Division of Archives and History.)

MAKING A LIVING

Abner fished to make a living. When fishing was good, he'd go every morning to set nets. Portsmouth was known for good fish, so boats would come through picking up the fish and paying the fishermen. Abner had a gas engine shove boat. He could pole it through shallows or power it across the sound.

He also worked taking care of the lighthouse that was in the sound between Portsmouth and Atlantic. He helped to keep the light going and helped keep up the buoys there at the lighthouse. They were big orange things anchored there. They had a horn that Abner kept operational.

He was not in the Coast Guard or the Lighthouse Service; he substituted when they needed help. Any job was good then. Just to be working was good. Sometimes Abner worked for no money. It was important to keep the lights going for the safety of all seamen.

Portsmouth was so far away from everything that there was no business other than fishing or working as a hunting guide. The Lifesaving Service, and later the Coast Guard, provided work for a few men. Portsmouth had been known as a port of entry for over 200 years. By the turn of the century [1900], few ships were using the Ocracoke Inlet. Engines were replacing sails and ships were going to large ports. So when the Depression came, we lost a lot of residents. Many

The Methodist Church was the heart of Portsmouth. It held everyone together in times of trouble, and provided a place to celebrate when things were going well. There was a special service on Christmas Eve. (Photo by Frances Eubanks.)

This photograph was made when Mary Snead Dixon visited her niece, Clara Gaskins, in Morehead City on June 3, 1985. (Courtesy Frances Eubanks private collection.)

The Methodist preacher came to the church about once a month. Afterward, he went to someone's house who wasn't a churchgoer.

Christmas was nothing outstanding except we had a beautiful tree at the church that had real candles on it. We would go on Christmas Eve and the candles would be lit. Gifts would be given out. I remember one year a feller from the Coast Guard Station played Santa. His jacket caught on fire.

SUPERSTITION

Most people were not superstitious although a few like Mr. Gilgo was superstitious about black cats. I remember him telling Abner that a black cat had crossed his path so he had to turn around and go back home. Abner didn't believe in them. Once I heard Steve Roberts say there was a witch on Portsmouth who could put spells on people. Back then many people believed in them. I didn't hear him say who it was, but I never believed in that kind of thing. Now, Atlantic was known to be a superstitious place.

WORLD WAR II

Having the Coast Guard in the old Lifesaving Station during World War II made everyone feel secure. With the war right there off the banks, it was the best thing that could have happened. They had lookouts all-day and regular patrols on the beach at night.

I left Portsmouth six months of the year because I didn't have any children to teach. It got to the point I could count the number on one hand because by then there were few children of the Coast Guardsmen.

I went to Salter Path to teach because fishing was on the "bum." And I wanted to

went to see if they could do better elsewhere.

When storms came, I could look out and see over 100 sailboats in the inlet. It was 40 miles across the Pamlico Sound to Washington, so many of the boats would come into the Portsmouth Harbor for safety. It was too risky to attempt sailing back across the sound.

RELIGION

Religion was a major part of everyone's life and a major part of our social life. There were plenty of stories about Mr. Betts, a preacher. He did all right here and wouldn't let his wife cook on Sunday. He ruled his family with an iron hand.

When fishing was on the "bum" and there was no longer a need for a teacher on Portsmouth, Mary Snead Dixon accepted a teaching job in Salter Path on Bogue Banks. Salter Path was not well populated in the 1940s and there were no paved roads. She caught the mail boat and spent six months a year teaching there and then returned to Portsmouth. After the hurricane, Abner decided to move with Mary. (Courtesy North Carolina Division of Archives and History.)

do what I could to help out. Mr. George Smith was carrying the mail to Morehead City and then to Salter Path. I heard they needed a teacher so I got Mr. Smith to take me. I think 1950 was the last year I taught there.

I tried to get Abner to go with me, but he stayed and waited for me to come back at the end of the term. The second year I was away, the worst storm hit the area and washed over Portsmouth. The ocean breakers came all the way over the village and washed through the window where my sewing machine was sitting in the dining room. The force was so strong that coffee was plastered to the ceiling. Water was standing 22 inches deep in the kitchen. Sarah's husband had a large boat and he brought what he could away. Up until then, we had felt pretty safe in Portsmouth. All the houses were 3 feet up and built to withstand storms. They had special storm doors with no screens that were thick and heavier than usual. Most had heavy shutters that would cover the windows.

After that storm, Abner was willing to move.

In the 1940s and early 1950s, when Mary Snead Dixon was teaching Salter Path, the community was an up-and-coming place. As Portsmouth was on the decline, the Bogue Banks beach areas were developing into the tourist attraction they are today. In 1945, there was a passable road, a movie theater, and a grocery store. (Courtesy Eubanks/Salsi private collection.)

Portsmouth, the coastal jewel, was the place of love, harmony, and neighbors helping neighbors. It still lives on in the hearts of former residents, descendents, and visitors. Even in the year 2000, Portsmouth is a place of mystery and by no means an easy place to visit. To get there, one has to launch a pre-planned expedition. Frances and I have yet to find a person who has been there who has not been dazzled by the sense of community even though no full time residents have lived there in over 30 years. This makes the stories of Clara Gaskins, Marian Babb, and Mary Snead Dixon even more important. They too were women ahead of their time. They were brave pioneers in the early 20th century who forged careers despite their isolation.

We are grateful and indeed lucky to know Connie Mason, who traveled to Columbia, South Carolina, and interviewed Frances's Aunt Mary Snead Dixon as part of an oral history project sponsored by the Cape Lookout National Seashore. Frances and her sister Barbara filled in many details about Mary Dixon. They remembered their mother, Clara Salter Gaskins, and grandparents very clearly and their additions concerning the Salter House was most valuable. Jessie Lee Babb Dominique was the last baby born in Portsmouth and helped clarify details from her sister, Marian's narrative. An afternoon visit with former resident Dot Willis provided great insight into daily life.

—Lynn Salsi

CHAPTER FIVE
DOWN EAST
MARY ELIZABETH MASON AND DOT WILLIS

GOING HOME

We grew up in very special places. Most of our young years were spent in Carteret County on Portsmouth or in Atlantic. For a while we lived in Oriental on the Neuse River and in Aurora near our mother's parents. Our various moves had significance and were for the good of the family. In fact, family was very important to our mother and father. We moved from Portsmouth to stay near our grandparents and once we moved so that Daddy could be in business with family members.

Education was an important part of our lives. We lived in Aurora so that I could attend high school and then we moved to Atlantic so that Mary Elizabeth could attend high school. By then, Atlantic High School had become known as the best school in the state and our father's parents were living close by.

We lived on Portsmouth twice. Daddy was born there in 1899 and was raised there. One thing was for sure, our daddy, Ben Salter, loved Portsmouth best of all. He talked about Portsmouth all of his life.

Our mother, Thelma Styron, was born in 1900 on Hog Island, which is a very small remote island near Cedar Island but it's farther away from the mainland in the Pamlico Sound. I visited Hog Island a few years ago. No one lives there anymore. I was surprised how small and bare it seemed. I wondered how in the world families chose to live there. But at the time, everyone had to be near the water so they could make a living and feed their families. Hog Island surely was good for being close to fishing.

Mama met Daddy on the mail boat as she was returning to Hog Island from school in Beaufort. The boat came from Beaufort, went to Atlantic, and then to Cedar Island, and on to Hog Island, and then to Portsmouth. The Lola Post Office was on Hog Island, so the mail boat stopped daily. My granddaddy, Mother's father, was the postmaster.

Ben Salter loved his family and he loved Portsmouth. He related stories to his children all of his life. He and Dot later wrote a book about his life on the island. He is shown here at the age of 16. (Courtesy Dot Willis private collection.)

Mama attended high school at St. Paul's in Beaufort. It was not unusual for families living in remote areas to send their children to the boarding school. Mrs. Geoffroy, the headmistress, was very, very strict and did not put up with any nonsense. She wouldn't let anyone get near her students. So when Daddy and Mama decided to get married, Daddy went to Mama's school and told Mrs. Geoffroy that he was her cousin. They ran off and got married. They went to Aurora, where Aunt Mamie lived. Then they went on to Elizabeth City and got married. We heard about how our granddaddy was out looking for Mama. He was worried to death when he heard that she left school.

After they married, Mama and Daddy moved to Portsmouth and had a little house next door to Daddy's parents. That's the way it was all of our young lives. We lived near family. It was good to grow up in a close, loving family. Our father and mother took an interest in us. We were told that Daddy named each one of the six children that came along.

Our sister, Ethel Marie, was born the next year, 1918, on Hog Island. Mama went home to her mama and a midwife helped take care of her and Ethel Marie. Ethel Marie came home to Portsmouth and then when I was born, Mama stayed on Portsmouth. Miss Chrissie Fulcher delivered me. I don't remember anyone ever saying that she was paid. I suppose she got supper and some fresh fish to take home with her. By the time Mary Elizabeth was born three years later, Daddy's parents had moved to Atlantic and we moved to be near them. Mary Elizabeth was born at home in Atlantic and Miss Nance was the midwife there.

From the late 1800s until the 1940s, it was not unusual for people to move back and forth between all the little Down East islands and villages. They all had names like Ocracoke, Cedar Island, Sea Level, Davis, Bettie, Smyrna, Otway, Gloucester. Many people from Portsmouth moved inland to be closer to conveniences and because hurricanes washed over the island. It was terrifying during severe storms to see the ocean meet the sound right in the middle of Portsmouth. There were no roads Down East and everyone had to have a boat. The waterways were our highways and most visiting was by boat. Many went to church by boat and most shopping was in small local general stores or by going to Beaufort.

Boats were used for making a living, for transportation, and sometimes for recreation. Boats were a way of life for everyone. Most men in Down East were commercial fishermen. That's how they fed their families and how they made a

Midwives delivered the babies in the rural Down East areas of North Carolina where there were few doctors and no hospitals. Mrs. Crissie Fulcher of Portsmouth delivered Dot Salter Willis. She is pictured with her husband, Manson Fulcher. (Courtesy Dot Salter Willis private collection.)

Dot and Mary Elizabeth shared many good times on Portsmouth at their grandparents' house. This photograph shows large wooden supports holding up the front porch. The image was taken before the wreck of the John I. Snow, *which was transporting lumber and supplies to build a hotel. John Wallace Salter, their grandfather, purchased pillars at salvage and replaced the old porch supports with beautiful, white, round columns. (Courtesy Dot Salter Willis private collection.)*

Fishing trawlers still dock at the same harbor in Atlantic where the mail boat used to come in—right beyond Winston Hill's Store. The dock is gone but the memories linger on. Many people came to visit this spot, where they had spent many hours waiting for a ride to another community. Often Atlantic was just a stop over place for those on their way to Portsmouth and Ocracoke. (Photo by Frances Eubanks.)

living. Fishing activity dictated the way others made their livelihood. At one time there were barrel makers, fishermen, fish house owners, net makers, and boat builders in almost every community. Back then there was also a need for watermen to haul fish up and down the waterways.

When we were small, the men used sailing skiffs for fishing. Gasoline engines were unheard of. I can remember when our uncle bought the first gasoline motor that anyone had ever seen. It was only a 3 horsepower Latham. He used it to power his skiff. It was a real curiosity. People stood around and enjoyed the sound it made. He was so proud of it that you'd have thought he was going to power a ship with only 3 horsepower.

Most fishing centered around the varieties that could be salted—always mullet and spot. There was no refrigeration, so fish that could be sold, shipped, or traded had to be preserved with salt. A lot of activity centered around the preparation of the fish after it was caught. They used handmade wooden barrels to place the fish and salt in. Once the fish were caught they were slit and cleaned. A layer of salt and then a layer of fish and a layer of salt and so on were placed in the barrel. Everyone had a barrel of salt fish on their porch. It was the main stay of our diets especially in the winter when the men weren't fishing and we couldn't grow a garden.

The fishermen would catch big mullet just for the roe. That was the best part of that kind of fish. In fact, not many people cared to eat the rest of the fish. Eating dried roe was popular. It was delicious. I expect it was as good to us as caviar is to other people. I remember the effort people made to put boards up all around outside to lay the roe on to dry in the sun. People with a two-story house would actually put roe up on the roof. They'd go upstairs and lean out of a dormer window and line roe on a sheet or board on the roof. Some people rigged mosquito netting around to keep off the insects. The greatest challenge though was in keeping cats away. If there was a cat anywhere around, there would be a problem. The cats loved roe, too. (Dot.)

SCHOOL DAYS

Our first memories of school were on Portsmouth. Mary Snead Dixon was our teacher. We walked each day to the one-room schoolhouse. Miss Mary had desks lined up row by row by grades. She spent the day teaching each separate age group represented in the school. Sometimes when Dot and I sit and talk, we remember some of the people. We can just see Lucille Fulcher Armstrong sitting in her desk sucking her thumb and twisting her hair. We remember Miss Mary coming to school with her own children, Felts and Bethenia. She taught her own children in the classroom with the rest of us.

Miss Mary was a good teacher but she didn't put up with any foolishness. She had to be strict because she was teaching too many grades and didn't have an assistant. There was no talking back and you better not get a whipping at school, because you'd get another whipping at home as well.

I smile when we think of Miss Mamie calling after her son, Lambert Morris Jr. We were living in Atlantic and we could always hear her. Wherever Lambert was, she was always calling after him saying, "Dahling, come home." We snickered every time we heard her say, "Dahling."

Mr. Morris, Lambert's father, was a judge and was well respected. (Mary Elizabeth.)

One day I was walking down the road singing and not thinking anyone was listening. The Judge came up and asked what I was singing. I said, "Barney Google cooked a cake. It give his horse a belly ache." It tickled him. Every time I saw him after that he would ask me to sing it or would ask me about Barney Google.

We walked by ourselves to school each day. On Portsmouth we walked from the lower end where we lived on Sheep Island. We walked with Donald Gilgo and met 45 or 50 other children at school. We carried a jar of water and something to eat. At lunchtime we went outside to eat. (Dot.)

Our lunch was always a biscuit and something between the biscuit. Sometimes we might have a streak of lean, but most often that something was a fried egg. To this day, Dot can hardly stand to look at a fried egg.

All of the school desks had inkwells. That was the perfect place for dipping another student's long hair while she was seated in front and facing forward. All kinds of other stuff went into the wells—especially spit balls. When we got to Atlantic, the inkwells were still on the desks, but by then we were using pencils and the wells were dry most of the time. You'd be surprised what might be stuffed inside.

When we got a break from our classes, we loved playing hopscotch. We drew our hopscotch pattern in the dirt with a stick. We could do that for hours. We played and had a good time with our friends and relatives. A bunch would get together and have some sort of adventure.

After school, we played hopscotch. We also played house and croquet. Our daddy put swings in the old oak trees. When we moved to Atlantic, before they put in the road, we had swings in the old trees at

Atlantic is located Down East on the coast of North Carolina. It is known for its charming harbor and easy access to the fishing grounds of the sounds and Atlantic Ocean. This c. 1948 photograph shows commercial wooden boats ready for the day's fishing. (Courtesy Billy Piner private collection.)

Uncle Kelly's house. The girls would get in the swings and the boys would push us so hard we'd go to the top of the tree. It'd scare us to death and we'd yell and holler.

We enjoyed exploring Atlantic and Uncle Dave had a cave on his land. There was a big bank in the sand and they dug it out. We could stand up in it. The boys especially liked playing in it. We went into it sometimes but it was not fun because it was dark and damp. (Mary Elizabeth.)

One thing was for sure, we were never bored and we never heard another child say, "I'm bored." I guess we knew better than to get bored. Our parents would'a found work for us to do. We were living in a time when children were to be seen and not heard. It was not unusual for our parents to take us visiting friends and relatives. Often we were expected to sit

quietly and listen while the adults did the talking.

Older people in our town, even those who were not related, might correct us and we were supposed to listen. We were taught respect and had to put a handle to everyone's name. If they were related, we called them Uncle and Aunt and otherwise it was Miss, Mrs., Mr. If the person was a close family friend, we might also address them as "Uncle" or "Aunt." No matter what we also lived by "the Golden Rule." (Dot.)

Many families had a lot of children. Therefore, five or six children in the same school could be related. I remember the Styron children went to school with us in Atlantic. They generally went to school by themselves, each one at the time. One day one of our relatives was watching first one and then another and then another of the children walk down the road toward to school. He looked up and said, "How many kids do they have living in that house?" Actually they only had six children. They were a great family. The children would get together and sing "You Are My Sunshine." It was beautiful!

When we were in school in Atlantic, we walked home for lunch. Our Cousin Irene had to come by bus from Cedar Island so she packed her lunch. She took the most unusual things we'd ever heard of. She'd have stewed squirrel or possum and always between a biscuit. She'd talk about what she was eating for lunch and I'd say, "Don't tell me anymore about it." (Mary Elizabeth.)

HOME WORK

We were expected to help around the house. Washing and ironing was a production. The clothes were washed in a pot in the yard. A fire was built under the pot so we could have hot water. We washed and rubbed on a board with a big bar of Octagon Soap. The procedure would take the skin off our fingers. If things were real dirty, we would have to rub and rub using lye soap. Now that would take the skin off your hands.

Then we had to hang the clothes. Shirts were always hung by clothespins at the seams at the tails. Dresses had to be hung by the shoulders, and pants were hung by the waist. When things were dry, we had to take them in and either fold or iron them.

We had two heavy flat irons that we would heat on the stove and use for ironing clothes. We'd go out to a cedar tree and pick small branches of the cedar. We put a paper bag on the ironing board and then we laid the cedar on top; then we'd set the hot iron on top of the branch. We ran the hot iron over the greenery as we ironed. The cedar acted as a type of starch and helped the clothes iron better—the iron would glide along.

Everything back then was made of cotton. We had to iron ourselves to death to get the wrinkles out.

There was also cooking, sweeping, dusting, and cleaning kerosene lampshades to do. We were expected to do our share of the housework. Since everything was done by hand—the washing, ironing, cooking we had to pitch in without being asked.

Our sister, Geraldine, would hold back sometimes if a new *True Story* magazine was out. She'd sit and read and read. I'd holler, "Come on, Geraldine." She'd still not come. I'd holler to Mama, "Mama, she's not coming." It's so funny how you fuss at each other as children. We mostly got along and always got over our aggravations. Geraldine was sweet and precious. (Mary Elizabeth.)

Mama could sew, and that is the reason we had nice clothes to wear. Actually, she was gifted; she could look at a picture in a catalogue or magazine and copy it. She'd take newspaper and cut out a pattern and then cut it out of fabric. She usually bought fabric from the Sears or Montgomery Ward catalogues.

She made Mary Elizabeth the prettiest white dress. It was a tradition that the juniors would sing to the seniors. The girls had to wear a white dress. Mary Elizabeth picked out a picture and Mama ordered the fabric. She made the dress and scalloped the hem. You'd a'thought it had come from New York City.

One other time Mary Elizabeth was wearing another pretty dress that Mama had made and we decided to go over to Grandmother's house to visit. She lived two or three houses down from us but we went a short cut through a little hammock through the woods. Just as Mary Elizabeth jumped across the ditch, she jumped right onto a skunk. That was really something—what a coincidence. That smell was so bad I can't describe it.

Atlantic Elementary School holds memories for many as one of the state's best schools. The school pictured above was built in the 1950s to replace the old three-story wooden structure where the Salter children and the Hill children attended. (Photo by Frances Eubanks.)

Clayton Willis is pictured here on a pony. Young people took pride in owning their own pony. Clayton lived on Portsmouth and was one of many young people who owned a Banker pony. (Courtesy Dot Salter Willis private collection.)

Mother washed and washed that dress but the smell was still in it. Someone told her if the garment was buried for awhile, the smell would leave it. She buried the dress and after a while dug it up and washed it again. When she put a hot iron on it, the smell was so strong we couldn't even stay in the house. I think she might have buried the dress again and left it there.

Considering the times in which we lived, we only had one broken bone in the family. Our younger sister was standing in the open back door of our house on Portsmouth. A wind came up and blew the door to, knocking my sister out into the yard. There were only three steps but the door was really heavy and the wind was forceful. Daddy heard her crying and went running. Mother said that Daddy ran around the house more than once in distress from hearing her cry. He took her by boat to Beaufort to get medical help and get the arm set. I can't imagine how traumatic that must have been for both of them. There our sister was in pain and Daddy trying to hurry in a sailboat.

Daddy loved horses. He rode with the many round-ups on the Banks. Sometimes these pennings were held every year. The horses were mostly from the old mustang breed that came ashore hundreds of years ago. But people also brought in horses from the mainland and they eventually got mixed with the wild horses. During the round-ups they'd corral the wild horses riding their own horses. The men would corral them and brand them. People

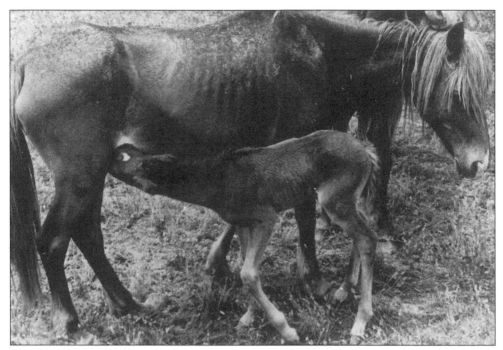

Pony pennings were part of life on the Banks. Portsmouth held annual roundups. Local people adopted ponies for their personal use. Some were taken by boat for use in other communities. Ben Salter owned many of the ponies throughout his life. When the government ordered the ponies off Portsmouth, Dot adopted two. (Courtesy North Carolina Division of Archives and History.)

would then adopt a certain number. My grandparents and daddy always had horses. Daddy used to tell us about riding up and down the beach. When he was young, they had the round-ups near his house. He would take a wild horse, break it, train it, and keep it for his own use. (Dot.)

FOOD

We butchered pigs in the fall. We took the fresh pork and cured it by salting it down in wooden barrels. We'd place layers of meat between lots of salt. When we ate the ham, we'd boil the salt out. Mason jars were useful for canning fruit, vegetables, and meat. Our parents and grandparents had chickens, so we ate a lot of eggs. We also ate fresh chicken and canned chicken. We rarely had fried chicken, but when we were going to have fried chicken, Daddy would pen the chicken, feed it corn, and then kill it. I have memories of a chicken running around with his head cut off. My daddy killed the chickens. The children's job was to pluck the feathers and then Grandmother would singe off the tiny feathers that weren't plucked.

Mama would cut up the chicken, salt it, and place it in clean Mason jars. The jars would be placed in a large pot of water and boiled until the chicken was cooked and the jars sealed. In the winter the canned chicken made the best pastry and chicken. (Dot.)

The fall of the year was the time for butchering. People in all of the rural Down East communities raised livestock. This photo was made on Portsmouth. (Courtesy Dot Salter Willis private collection.)

Cattle sales were a common sight in the 1930s and 1940s in coastal North Carolina. The one shown here was held in 1942. The buyers and sellers were gathered in Beaufort. (Courtesy North Carolina Department of Archives and History.)

When we were living in Atlantic, Dot decided to take care of some chickens. We named each one and they were kind'a like pets. When Daddy killed them to eat, we got so upset we walked over to our grandmother's house to find something to eat. (Mary Elizabeth.)

We ate a lot of ducks and geese during the winter hunting season. We also ate fried duck eggs. Mama used duck eggs in making cakes from scratch. People also salted fowl and shipped them off the island in barrels.

We helped pluck the feathers and saved all of them to use in pillows and mattresses. If we didn't need them, we shared them or saved them. The wings of the fowl were used as feather dusters. They were left just the way they were. Then we dried them out awhile before we used them for dusting.

We had to buy or trade for our flour, corn, molasses, sugar, coffee, and such. In Atlantic, we'd get supplies from Mr. Winston Hill's store. We bought molasses from a barrel for 5¢ per pint. Mr. Hill's store had a little bit of everything. (Dot.)

MOVING

Moving was a decision of our parents. We knew it was best for our family. The two times we moved from Portsmouth, we picked up everything we could and put it on a boat and went to Atlantic. We had to have a table, chairs, beds, kerosene stove and kerosene lamps.

We moved to Oriental by truck. We loaded everything up and the truck drove over very rutted roads.

Daddy's parents decided to leave Atlantic and move to Oriental. Daddy, Uncle Tom, and Granddaddy thought it was a good idea to go over there and run a fish house. They opened a place. For a while, they fished and also bought fish

from other fishermen. We had a good time in Oriental. Everything was much the same as in Atlantic, except everything didn't center around fishing. They had some lumbering and a sawmill there. (Dot.)

ENTERTAINMENT

When we were little, Daddy talked about how the people on Portsmouth could go over to the old Marine hospital and make music. Someone had a guitar and someone had a fiddle. Mr. Jesse Babb went and played and they held a dance. In fact, he told us about Walter Howard and his brother Edgar who left Ocracoke and went to New York to appear in vaudeville and later with Gene Autry. They were Daddy's good friends. He enjoyed remembering their talents.

I'll never forget the one time Daddy took me to Ocracoke for a square dance. He was asked to call the dance so he let me go with him while he called. He took me in the boat. I remember being scared going across the inlet. It was a big deal for a little girl.

Grandmother had an old gramophone that sat on a box. It was one that had a big horn on top. It played cylinders not records. People would come over to her house and dance. Daddy'd get up and really cut a step. (Dot.)

When we were older, on dates we walked, talked, and visited with friends. Atlantic had a small theatre and we enjoyed movies when we could get the money. Whenever we came home at night, we were expected to get the pans of bread Mama left rising on the mantle piece down and shape it into rolls. We'd fix the pans to rise overnight and Mama would cook them for breakfast the next morning. We'd have enough rolls left over for lunch and dinner.

Winston Hill's Store was the center of activity for the village of Atlantic. It was an old-time general store that sold just about anything and everything. Young people gathered to hear the latest tunes on the juke box and to drink soda and eat ice cream. (Courtesy Mary Elizabeth Mason private collection.)

During high school we had the best time going to Mr. Winston's store. All the crowd went there. He had booths and a jukebox. We'd sit in the booth and listen to music. We'd eat ice cream—either chocolate or vanilla and drink Orange Crush in the brown bottle. They were a nickel apiece. Sometimes boys would come in and we would sit and talk. Daddy would give me a dime and I'd have so much fun. (Mary Elizabeth.)

If we could get Daddy to give us a quarter, we'd have a wonderful time. If he'd caught fish that week, we'd get the quarter.

Daddy did so many things to make a living. He served in the Coast Guard, fished commercially, and ran a hunting club on Portsmouth called the Salter Gun Club. Daddy carried Babe Ruth, the famous baseball player out hunting. (Dot.)

CHRISTMAS

Wherever we were living, Christmas was special. We always had a Christmas tree. We would go out and find the very prettiest cedar tree. We made chains with different colored loops from construction paper; we threaded popcorn into a long chain. We always received gifts—a little bit of something. The girls got a little doll and the boys got a knife. One Christmas my doll had a china head and hands and a stuffed body.

We always went to a special Christmas service at church. Christmas on Portsmouth was probably the most fun. We always hunted for the best cedar tree

Dot and Mary Elizabeth remember fondly their Aunt Pearl, their daddy's sister. She was married in 1917 in the Methodist church on Portsmouth. Stories of her beautiful, big wedding were passed down through the family. She was once voted the "Most Beautiful Woman" in Carteret County. (Courtesy Dot Salter Willis private collection.)

to decorate. All of the aunts and uncles who had moved from Portsmouth would come back. It was so exciting. They would bring a small gift for everyone.

Aunt Pearl would bring real candles that would clip onto the tree. We would only be allowed to light them just for a little while. There was a great fear of fire. Burning candles, especially on a tree, had to be watched carefully. (Dot.)

I remember spending Christmas in Oriental. They still believed in Old Christmas, and we were told that the cows bowed down at midnight. Of course, we went out to see if that was true. There we were out in a cow pasture. We looked closely and even at midnight we didn't see a cow bow.

The old train from New Bern would stay in Oriental overnight. They'd leave the engine puffing all night long until they took off the next morning. On New Year's Eve, we got up in the engine, rang the bell, and blew the whistle at midnight.

Many New Years we got in the back of a truck. Then we went down the road slamming and banging pots, pans, and lids together to make all the noise we could make. (Mary Elizabeth.)

FROM DIRT TO PAVEMENT

Dirt roads from the other communities to Atlantic got paved. Roads opened Down East to the world. Grandmother had a huge grapevine in her backyard. I came home from school and a man was cutting the vines so a road could go through. He was painting it with a liquid and when I asked why, he said it was so

When Highway 70 was cut from Beaufort to Atlantic, it opened up all of the little villages along the way. The Atlantic harbor became a bustling place for boats and cars in the 1940s. (Courtesy North Carolina Department Archives and History.)

the vine wouldn't bleed to death. They also came and cut down some of the big oaks where our swings were hanging. They cut a road down to the water and then cleared enough for a turntable. That's what we called the area for the cars to turn around.

Before then the few roads were dirt and were deeply rutted and those with cars couldn't travel very far. I remember that the North River bridge was wooden. As we crossed in Uncle Tom's car, the boards would pop up and down.

Uncle Tom had one of the first cars in the area. It wasn't long after that that having a car was "the thing." I can remember the first car we ever had. Miss Adeline ran the first taxi service. During the war she charged $5.00 round trip and

carried a carload of people to Beaufort for shopping. She waited until everyone had finished their errands and then brought everyone back to Atlantic. (Mary Elizabeth.)

CHURCH

Grandmother and grandfather went to church on Cedar Island to the Primitive Baptist Church. Father was the last deacon in the church. The Primitive Baptists were among the very first religious groups who came to the Down East area. They were called "hardshelled." We went to church but they didn't have a Sunday school. They expected their members to be devout and committed. If

The Salters were Primitive Baptists. Dot remembers her father going across the Pamlico Sound by boat from Portsmouth to attend church on Cedar Island. When the family moved to Atlantic, they attended the Hunting Quarters Primitive Baptist Church. (Photo by Frances Eubanks.)

people were not totally dedicated, they were referred to as "leaners." In other words, they weren't really of the church they just leaned toward it.

The Primitive Baptists did not believe in being missionary minded. They thought those who wanted to join should come to them. New members had to have a vision and be voted into the congregation. Then they'd baptize the new members in Core Sound. I don't think there are many members left in our area anymore. I think a few other churches still baptize in the Sound.

Once a lady came to our community from some place up north. She was going around asking questions and making lists of unusual names. She spoke to Dr. Paul in Sea Level, the community closest to

Atlantic. He told her that there were three people's names that ran him crazy. He said, "They are Sorrowful Emery, Increase Willis, and Afenbin."

We'd go to church on Sunday and we'd look in our songbook and giggle when we thought of a man we knew named Loami Gaskill. The song was "Lo I Am With You." We always wondered if that was how Loami got his name. We never got to ask, but later he changed his name to "Carl." (Mary Elizabeth.)

MARRIED LIFE

My mother-in-law was a very special lady. Her name was Amelia Mason and everybody always called her Meelie.

Hunting Quarters Primitive Baptist Church was so named because it was organized in 1780, when the village was still known as Hunting Quarters. Some say that the church was actually the first church built in Sea Level. Although there are no active members, the church still sits in repose off of the main road. (Photo by Frances Eubanks.)

The mother of 16 children, Mrs. Amelia Mason was called "Miss Meelie" by family and friends. For years, she and her husband kept the Pilentary Hunting Club on Core Banks and then later settled in Atlantic. (Courtesy Mary Elizabeth Mason private collection.)

She had 16 children and knew a lot of things. When it was time to have her first child, she and her husband were out on Core Banks at the Pilentary Hunting Club, where Mr. Alvin was working as a caretaker. It was about 10 miles down the banks from Portsmouth. The weather had been brutal and there were constant freezing temperatures. When it was very close to the time the baby was coming, the sound was totally frozen. There was no way she could go by boat to her mother's. Mr. Alvin bundled her up and put her in the boat. He and some others walked and pushed the boat across the ice and got Miss Meelie to the midwife in time.

She told me one time that when she went to bed at night she had one baby right here and patted her stomach. She said that there was another baby between her and Mr. Alvin and one in a cradle at the foot of the bed." She was remarkable and had raised so many children she learned not to get too worried. She was quick as a lick and was quite a woman. We got along really well and she never gave me any advice.

One day my little boy, Larry, swallowed a penny. I was so upset and didn't know what to do and then I saw Miss Meelie walking by my house going to the store. I called out, "Miss Meelie, my young'un swallowed a penny." She didn't miss a beat; she called back to me, "Forget it. It'll come out." She just kept on walking. (Mary Elizabeth.)

WORLD WAR II

I graduated from high school in May of 1941. By then Monroe had rejoined the Coast Guard. He came home to get me and we went to Elizabeth City and got married on the way to New York where he was stationed. When war was declared in

Monroe Mason enlisted in the Coast Guard at 17. When he completed his tour, he returned to Atlantic and attended high school to finish his education. He and Mary Elizabeth Salter struck up a friendship and he told her that he was back in school to be close to her. That was the beginning of their love story. Monroe re-enlisted in the Coast Guard in 1941, and when Mary Elizabeth graduated from high school, he came to "get her." They were married, and when World War II broke out later that year, he was stationed on a ship that was sent overseas. Here he is looking handsome in his uniform in the 1940s. (Courtesy Mary Elizabeth Salter Mason private collection.)

The skills of net making and net hanging (as seen here) are as old as the art of fishing. Skilled net makers were in demand in the late 1800s and early 1900s on the coast. Residents in the Down East villages recall their parents making and repairing nets.

December, he made arrangements to send me home to Atlantic so he would know I was safe. It was a sinking feeling knowing there was a war and my husband was sure to be sent overseas.

Shortly after coming home, my aunt asked me to drive to Maine to carry my uncle who was stationed there. I was happy to go with her and we made plans to stop in New York to see my husband. When we got there, we found that his ship had been sent to North Africa under sealed orders. I was so upset.

We knew about the war. We didn't have a radio and Daddy would say, "I got to go down to hear the radio." He'd go down to the store where people gathered and listen to Gabriel Heater. The news was very important. He'd come back home and we were all eager to hear what was going on. He'd say, "Oh, it's bad." Our hearts would sink. We looked forward to him saying, "Things look good."

Dot's husband, Joe, volunteered to serve and joined the Coast Guard. During the war, the Navy took over the Coast Guard so our husbands were assigned to navy ships.

I stayed in Atlantic all during the war. We had blackouts and there was constant talk of boats being bombed right off of our coast.

During the last of the Depression and during the war, my mother-in-law, Meelie, tied nets to make a little money. Atlantic had a net house. She went to the net house and worked. They needed everyone they could get to make nets so they had many people in homes making the nets. I tied them for fun because everybody else was doing it. They brought supplies to me and I was paid by the pound.

Each net was a different gauge. The net house furnished a piece of smooth wood to use to measure the gauge. The twine was wrapped around the wood. I'd slip so many "marshes" (meshes) until the wood piece was full. I'd slip it off and start again. It was fun to do and one of the few things women could do at the time to make a little extra money.

Dot Salter Willis (left) and Mary Elizabeth Salter Mason (middle) are pictured with Mary Elizabeth's daughter, Gaye. They attended the biannual Portsmouth Island Reunion, sponsored by the Friends of Portsmouth Island, in 2000. Descendents, friends, and visitors come together for a service in the Methodist church and have dinner on the grounds. (Photo by Frances Eubanks.)

The war years were very hard. My husband was away and then there was the worry about what was going to happen. I saved all the letters he sent me. We stayed at home in Atlantic and did the best we could. We had to use ration stamps to get sugar, coffee, and shoes. (Mary Elizabeth.)

I was at Carolina Beach when the war ended. Everybody was running around hugging and kissing each other and there were fireworks. (Dot.)

EDITOR'S NOTE

It was a great pleasure to talk with sisters who share the love of family and fond memories of a close and happy childhood.

I first met Dot four years ago at the Friends of Portsmouth Island Reunion.

Everyone looks forward to hearing her give the history of Portsmouth at every reunion. I knew immediately that she was someone I wanted to talk with. It was not until the reunion of 2000 that I had the opportunity to see Dot again. After the visit to Portsmouth, I rode the boat back to Ocracoke seated beside Dot's sister, Mary Elizabeth. I was fascinated by her stories of her mother-in-law, "Miss Meelie," and her memories of Atlantic. I aggravated Frances for two months to set up a meeting, for the two ladies are in fact Frances's cousins.

The pleasure has been all mine. Now, I have great memories of pleasant hours spent with the sisters talking about their wonderful families and their childhood memories.

—Lynn Salsi

CHAPTER SIX
ATLANTIC
WINSTON HILL

A LITTLE VILLAGE DOWN EAST

I was born and grew up in Atlantic, a little village Down East of Beaufort, on the banks of Core Sound. There was no better place to be then and even today there is no better place than Atlantic. It's small but it's home. I've been many other places and it was natural to come home again and to stay.

The Hill family came to Eastern North Carolina back in the late 1700s. Wise Hill settled in the Williston area, which is a small Down East community. At some point in the early 1800s, two of his sons, Peter and John Hill, moved to Atlantic. That's where my great-grandfather George Washington Hill was born and where he stayed. My family has been here ever since.

My mother was a college graduate. She was born and raised in the little village of Nebo, which is near Morganton in the western part of the state. Her sister had been recruited by the Atlantic school board to come and teach in the Atlantic school system. When she graduated, her sister talked her into moving Down East to keep her company and to also teach at the school. Back then, she and her sister were brave to move so far from their family. But they did and they were excellent schoolteachers.

My mother gave up teaching when she married my father. I never heard how they met and courted, but in such a small place, meeting was probably easy. I was always very close to my mother. She was very intelligent, loving, and mild mannered. She loved her family.

THE STORE

My father, Winston Hill, built his store in 1936. It was operated until 1985. You might say that I was born into the business, for I was born the year the store was built. He bought the property from Uncle Joe Mason. I understand that an old

The mail boat from Atlantic to Ocracoke was a daily sight in 1950. This photograph taken by a passenger shows the boat heading out from Atlantic with its load of mail bags. (Courtesy North Carolina Department of Archives and History.)

two-story store was once on the site. The warehouse, which is what we called the big back room built onto the back of our store, was built on the foundation of that old store. There was nothing fancy about the building. It was symmetrical front and back with two back doors and two front doors. The store was built after the road connected Atlantic to the rest of Carteret County, and my father didn't have to depend on boats to deliver his merchandise.

I think Uncle Joe's old store probably was closer to the dock than ours, so he could easily receive his merchandise via boat. That was the way things were in the days before roads were built. I know that Clayton Fulcher's present seafood business is on the bank where the original shoreline was. In the 1930s they built the present harbor that is still there today by pumping hydraulic fill.

While my parents were building their business in a general store, I had many good times with my friends, and of course, when I was old enough, I had to carry my weight at the store. By that time there was a large grocery store down the road, and there was less call for things in a small general store. The mail boat had long stopped operating, and those on their way up and down Highway 70 generally brought what they needed with them when they were on their way to catch the ferry on Cedar Island.

I have many fond memories of my time in Daddy's store and of the people who shopped there. We had many regular patrons and people'd stop in for something to take to eat to on the mail boat as they traveled between Atlantic, Ocracoke, and Portsmouth. The mail boat came in just down the street and behind

ESTABLISHED 1890

Southern Bargain House
THE HOUSE THAT BARGAINS BUILT

AGENTS FOR
ARISTOCRAT HOSIERY
BLUE RIDGE OVERALLS
BIG BEN OVERALLS
PRESIDENT WORK SHIRTS
HANES UNDERWEAR
NEW YORKER DRESS SHIRTS'

WONDER WEAR SHOES
RHINO SHOES

IMPORTERS OF
TOYS
NOVELTIES
FANCY GOODS
CROCKERY
CUTLERY
FLOOR COVERING

DISTRIBUTORS
"DOLLY DIMPLE"
BEAUTY PREPARATIONS

Wholesale Department Store,
Notions, Hosiery, Underwear Etc.

TELEPHONE 3-9085   RICHMOND, VA.   Mar. 16, 1938

SOLD TO

Winston Hill   36

TERMS: 2% 10 DAYS OR DUE NET   May 16, 1938   Atlantic, N. C.

Order No. 207

238E	1 dz	Baseball Caps		2 00
Seconds	2 dz	" "	1 25	2 50
				$4.50
				26
	Postage & Insurance			$4.76

Salesmen made the long trip by mail boat to call on Mr. Hill. Winston Hill has fond memories of the gentlemen who spent their entire careers going from place to place. The bill above was found in the attic of the old store. The prices certainly reflect a "change in the times." (Courtesy Winston Hunter Hill.)

the store to a dock on the sound. Winston Hill's also served as the bus station for the Seashore Transportation Company. Even though the mail boat was close by everyday, I never got to go on it. We'd sometimes swim off the mail boat after it came in from Ocracoke. But I never got a ride.

By 1936 the mail truck came into Atlantic from Beaufort. It would head Down East and would stop in all the little communities along the way that had a post office. It'd stop in Smyrna, Marshallberg, and others as it headed to Atlantic and then on to Cedar Island and back to Beaufort. When it arrived at the Atlantic Harbor, mail bags were loaded onto the mail boat to be delivered to Ocracoke and Portsmouth. Steve Stanley ran the mail truck for many years. In addition to the mail, he would often bring various people's filled prescriptions with him, as there were no drugstores in the little communities.

I didn't see as much of my mother as I would have liked when I was really little. She worked very hard in the store with my father and hired a babysitter for me. Agnes Styron was my sitter until I got up a little in age. Later, she went and worked at the Sanitary Restaurant in Beaufort. She worked there forever.

THE MARINES ARRIVE

When I was six years old, Atlantic Field was built. It changed Atlantic. Our little village was full of contractors and workmen rolling around with big equipment. It was something exciting. The base was built to train World War II pilots. There was a need to have an airfield close to the ocean to help patrol

The aerial photograph of Atlantic Field shows the size of the wartime project. (Photo from National Archives; loaned by Winston Hill.)

for U-Boats. Before that time, Atlantic was a sleepy little hamlet—a good place to live but not much excitement.

World War II certainly changed all that. As the runway and base facilities were being built, ships were burning off our coast from being torpedoed. Sometimes one would burn for days. Sometimes we couldn't swim in the sound because of the crude oil that was seeping from the ships and floating to shore. The shoreline would be covered with the oil.

During the war, Atlantic Field was a full-fledged airbase. They had housing, a hospital, a theatre, and recreation facilities.

A group of us would sneak out to the base to watch the planes take off and land. We'd watch them target practice. There was a bunker at the end of the runway and

they'd fire into it. They also used it to adjust their gun sights and range.

We were known to occasionally take home a few souvenirs of ammunition we found around that bunker. We'd go home, pull the heads off, dump the powder out, and set it on fire. I was much older when I realized that most of the shells we had were live. We could have been killed. But we weren't. Someone was watching over us.

The base was a U.S. Marine facility and was used for flight training. It was not unusual to see or hear a crash. In fact, a crash boat crew was stationed at the dock to help with rescues. Once two planes collided in mid-air and one of the engines fell in front of Mr. Lionel's house. Another one bellied into the deep sand at White Point. They just came out, jacked her up, and rolled her down the road, and took her back to the base.

CUTTING SCHOOL

I went to the old school in Atlantic. It was three floors with the younger grades on the bottom. In 1950 a new school was built and I entered the eighth grade.

My friends and I particularly liked to sneak out of school and swim in the canals that were on the military property. They intersected near a runway and formed a sizeable water hole. In order to get there we had to succeed in sneaking out of school. The old Atlantic School was near the field. We'd sneak out of the side door and then go about 100 feet. Next, we'd slide through the woods. The big trick was in sneaking across the baseball diamond on the military property without being detected. Once there, we had to crawl through a large drainage crock (pipe) that went all the way under the runway. It was dark, damp, and usually had water in it. We had to crawl about 30 feet in darkness before the crock took a 45-degree turn and we could see

The Atlantic Boat Basin provides a safe harbor for many commercial fishing boats. The fishing tradition lives on in this small community located on Core Sound. (Photo by Frances Eubanks.)

daylight. When we reached the turn, we still had a short distance to go. When we came to the end, we still had to crawl on our bellies through the sand. When we got to our secret swimming hole, we'd go skinny-dipping.

All of us had some fear of being caught. We knew that we'd probably get a nice stick across our back ends if we didn't walk the straight and narrow. Actually the stick was a sort of narrow paddle. Once we sneaked away at lunchtime. A whole bunch of us headed straight behind the school, then over the hill behind the cemetery, down the shell road toward Highway 70 and into the woods. We'd go there to hang out and to climb trees. We should have gone on back to school but we couldn't resist. We stayed out playing and didn't go back. The principal was living in the teacherage and had gone

home for dinner. He must have been running a little late. On his way back to school, he cut through the woods where we were. I can still remember being up in that tree and looking down and thinking, "oops." There stood the school principal looking up at us. He marched us all back to school and straight to his office. We had to bend over a desk to get whacked maybe three or four times. It was not meant to be brutal; it was supposed to be just enough to wake us up.

I didn't get whacked often, yet I was always getting caught doing something. It was all in fun. When I was in sixth or seventh grade, I used to catch green snakes. Sometimes I would stick one inside of my shirt and go into the classroom. When it would stick its head out of my shirt and someone would see it, the entire class would go wild. The

The old oak trees in Atlantic bring back memories of games, of climbing, and of swinging. Today, a line of oaks still grace the water's edge and overlook Core Sound. (Photo by Frances Eubanks.)

teacher would give me a lecture and ask me to take the snake outside.

As kids, we had great fun roaming around Atlantic. We liked climbing and hanging out of the old oak trees. We liked eating acorns. They were very good if we could find enough of them without worms. We also liked to eat chinquapins. The fruit is about the size of an acorn and has a thorny cover that has to be cracked off of it. It's a pity that they are not around much anymore.

AMBITION

While I was growing up, my parents were working very hard to build a business. I could always find them at the store. When I was old enough to sweep or run errands, I was put to work. When my older brother Neil went into the Air Force in 1950, my daddy really put me to work. While my friends were partying, I was working, and often they were having their fun at Winston Hill's store. I was the one serving them soft drinks. There was no excuse for me not being at work. I worked everyday after school, all day on Saturdays, and all through the summer vacation.

When I was in high school, I added two additional jobs. The day I turned 16, I got my driver's license and the next day I got my bus license. I drove the bus to Cedar Island to pick up students and then drove it back again after school to take them back home. I did this everyday until I graduated for $1.00 a day or $20.00 per month.

I also became the projectionist at the little local theater. Sterling Robinson owned the theater. It was one of the few things to do in town, had good popcorn, and was a popular place to be. I worked five shows a week Thursday, Friday, and Saturday. I took care of the film, got the projectors ready and ran the film. I saw so many movies in those years that I really saw nothing. I sat there looking at movie after movie and nothing went in unless it was loud or a very dramatic moment. One time I took a girlfriend up and forgot that the windows in the projection booth opened out toward the street. There I was in the booth with a girl and those outside who noticed were looking in. I found out when I got kidded. I was more careful after that..

Fishing was the business that most people in our area were engaged in. Before the store was built, my father fished as did my grandfather, and Uncle Marvin. My father had a freight boat converted to a trawler. My oldest brother, Roderick, fished before he became a merchant seaman. At one time I tried it out. Commercial fishing is the hardest work and the most dangerous work imaginable. I learned I was not man enough to be a fisherman and that I needed to seek my fortune elsewhere.

THE OLD WAY

I was fortunate enough to grow up witnessing many of the old ways and at the same time I experienced the full impact of modern changes. I remember watching Grandma Medora make her soap in a big iron pot. In fact, through the process I got to eat good cracklings, especially when she used bay leaves. The cracklings came when she'd try the fat meat. When the lard cooked out, she strained off the particles. The strained particles were set aside and were delicious. When the liquid fat cooked, it solidified and we used it for cooking. We saved our grease and that was what was eventually used in the soap.

When she got enough, Grandma got a can of Red Devil Lye and fixed it in the proper proportions for lye water. She blended in the fat and stirred it outdoors over a fire until it was right. She made it so many times that she just knew when it was ready. Next, she poured the liquid into molds and let it cool until it solidified. Now, that soap would give a good cleansing.

FOOD TO EAT

Our main diet was mostly what we could catch, including fish, oysters, shrimp, and scallops. In the old days we raised a hog or two. Everyone had a garden. We sold seed and fertilizer at the store. Most people had apple trees and pecan trees in their yards. When the vegetables came in, there was a lot of canning. Everyone canned beets, corn, tomatoes, beans, and made cucumber pickle. Those fresh canned vegetables were so delicious in the winter. I remember selling Straight 8 cucumber seeds and Golden Bantam corn seed. Everyone grew their salad greens. We'd mix kale, rape, and turnip seeds together.

In the fall, everyone would salt fish. We sold empty 50¢ lard cans and salt. Everyone would prepare their fish so they would have them to eat during the winter. It was much cheaper to salt the fish in the can. To fix them in wooden barrels would have been a great deal more expensive. Anyway, the wooden tubs usually held either 25 or 50 pounds. Even though cans rust, the salt fish were meant to be eaten within a few months.

BACK HOME

Between 1955 and 1959, I left Atlantic to serve in the Air Force. When I was discharged, I returned home and went to work full-time in the store. As the years went on, each of my brothers came into the business. It was a good thing to share what Daddy and Mama had worked years building up. It was a good place to be. I wish I had set up a tape recorder so we

This photograph captures the charm and elegance of Down East life. (Photo by Frances Eubanks.)

could still hear all the stories that were told in that place.

We sold about everything one could imagine in Winston Hill's store. We had fabric, bolts of Dan River, ribbon, marine hardware, shotgun shells, automotive supplies, groceries, produce, fresh meat, fish, decoys, clothing, penny candy, Green River chef knives—anything in the world you could think of.

We sold clothing and gear for commercial fishermen. We ordered gloves by the bale from M.L. Snyder. They weighed between 200 and 300 pounds. At one time, we sold more Ericsson oil skins (foul-weather gear) than any other store they supplied. When Carl Ericsson came to Boston to the fish expo, he came on down here to Atlantic to see us. He said that he wanted to visit the place that had

sold so much of his oil skins. He came and presented us with a fish filet knife.

We had a juke box and booths along the wall. People came in to enjoy a soda or have an ice cream cone. For years Winston Hill's was the gathering place. We also had a large back room—back beyond the groceries and the meat counter. That's where we sold plumbing supplies, paint, wet weather gear, and nails.

The most important place in the store was around the old round kerosene stove. It was there from the day the store was first built. Men would come in and stand around or sit around and talk. Now, they told some tales. We didn't have chairs so some would pull up a few old produce crates to sit on.

In the old days my parents sold a lot of things out of barrels. We had 100-pound bags of feed that came in beautiful print fabric that ladies used to sew into clothing. Molasses came in 55-gallon steel drums. We sold dill pickles out of a big jar for a nickel. We also sold mullet roe. Tilman Taylor specialized in curing roe and was big in salt mullet that we referred to as corned mullet. He packed the fish in salt in wooden tubs and sold them to wholesalers. He ran a route all up in Fayetteville and Kinston.

I remember the old-time salesmen. Preston Midgette was a salesman for Virginia-Carolina Hardware Company. He was from Oriental and worked out of Richmond, Virginia. He called on my father regularly. He'd come on the mail boat from Beaufort. The road didn't come through to Atlantic until 1936. Prior to that time everything had to be delivered by boat.

During World War II, my father had a hard time supplying the store. Henry Nesbitt furnished him chickens and Hilda Brown Bertrum furnished him milk. It was raw milk but was the only milk he could get. The White Ice Cream people got the state inspector on Daddy. Now Daddy had a temper. The inspector came on a surprise visit and Daddy caught him snooping in the cooler box. Daddy got real mad and locked him in for a while. Needless to say, Daddy would never do business with the White Ice Cream Company.

Father'd wheel and deal. During the war, he sometimes managed to get things his customers needed. When he got lard or sugar, he would hide it and keep it for his good customers. Everything was rationed—gas, tires, shoes, coffee, sugar. It was hard on the store owners and on the customers.

After the war, Daddy got Mr. Barnes with Maola Milk to agree to come and furnish the store with milk and ice cream. He agreed and until the day the store was closed, Winston Hill did business with Maola.

I was at the store long enough to see buying habits change. In the thirties and forties, my father bought cloth diapers case after case and sold them by the dozens. When disposable diapers first came out, we couldn't give them away. I remember several boxes sitting around for years. But in the sixties, when disposable diapers caught on, we couldn't give the cloth diapers away.

The good old days of the general store came to an end; by that time I had begun another endeavor. It was probably hardest on my mother when the store closed. She lived to be 92. About a year before she died, she said that she hated to see the store looking so run down. She said she would like to see it with a coat of paint. My brother and I went over and painted the store one more time, so that mother could see it looking as fresh and clean as it was in 1936.

Winston Hunter Hill is shown here at Winston Hill's store, the famous meeting place. (Photo by Frances Eubanks.)

EDITOR'S NOTE

Winston Hunter Hill took time from his very busy schedule to share memories of Atlantic. His love for and enthusiasm for his community shines through his every description and memory. It is clear that he loves his home. He is indeed a storyteller and historian. His jovial humor and dynamic personality can literally be felt while reading his story.

Throughout his life, Winston has steadfastly served his community and his county, helping to establish one of the first volunteer fire departments chartered under the state.

We are grateful that Winston shared a look into his family's store, which was a Down East landmark for many years. It has been a pleasure to share his love of Atlantic.

—Lynn Salsi

This scene of the Down East waterfront was typical of 1943. The nets are neatly spread on the netspreads that line the shore. At the end of the day, many boats were pulled up

on the shore awaiting the next day's activities. (Courtesy North Carolina Department of Archives and History.)

Boatbuilding was part of every Down East community. Many watermen constructed their own vessels in their yards. Most local boats were built by "rack of the eye" construction with no blueprints or plans. (Photo by Frances Eubanks.)

ABOUT THE AUTHOR

Lynn Salsi is dedicated to recording North Carolina history in children's books, non-fiction accounts, and historical fiction. Her plays for children have been produced in North Carolina, Washington, D.C., Baltimore, New York City, and London, England. She is well known for enrichment presentations in schools and colleges.

Lynn enjoys viewing history through the eyes of those who have lived it. She lives in Greensboro with her husband and two children. She is active in arts in education, the Piedmont Children's Book Festival, and Boy Scouts and loves inspiring children to write.

ABOUT THE PHOTOGRAPHER

Frances Eubanks photographs have been featured in books, museums, touring shows, and have been included in permanent collections. Her work has appeared on magazine covers and in magazine and newspaper articles. Frances has spent 30 years as an award-winning professional photographer. Her awards have been many and have placed her work on covers and in shows for the Core Sound Waterfowl Museum and the North Carolina Seafood Festival. She is dedicated to preserving North Carolina visual history. She lends her vast personal "first-person" knowledge of coastal history to her images. Frances lives with her husband in Newport and has two children and two grandchildren.

Frances and Lynn share a passion for recording the history of elder citizens in words and photographs, so "their stories will never be lost." They are the recipients of the Willie Parker Peace History Book Award from the North Carolina Society of Historians for *Images of America: Carteret County* (Arcadia Publishing).